Religion AND Life

Second Edition

VICTOR W. WATTON

Hodder & Stoughton

A MEMBER OF THE HODDER HEADLINE GROUP

ACKNOWLEDGEMENTS

The publishers would like to thank the following for permission to reproduce material in this book:

Extracts reproduced from P Bowen (Ed) *Themes and Issues in Hinduism*, 1998, and E Stuart *Religion is a Queer Thing*, 1997 by permission of Cassell, Wellington House, 125 Strand, London WC2R 0BB, England; Extracts from *The Alternative Service Book 1980* is copyright © The Central Board of Finance of the Church of England and is reproduced by permission; *Social Trends 28*, Crown Copyright 1999 is reproduced with permission of the Office for National Statistics; Geoffrey Chapman, an imprint of Cassell & Co, for extracts from *Catechism of the Catholic Church*; Christian Aid for extracts from their news release *Peace ambassador John Barnes flies back from Burundi*, 3 June 1998; Christian Education Movement for the extracts from *What Churches Say*, 2nd edition; Christian Research for the table from *UK Christian Handbook 1996/7*; HarperCollins Publishers Ltd for the extract from *A Backdoor to Heaven* by Lionel Blue; Hodder & Stoughton Educational for extracts from *Guidelines for Life* by Mel Thompson; The Islamic Society of North America for an extract from *A Handbook of Marriage*; Islamic Texts Society for the extract from *Muhammad his life based on the earliest sources* by M Lings, 1983; Muslim Educational Trust for the extracts from *What does Islam Say?* by Ibrahim Hewitt, 3rd edition, 1998; Extracts from *The Spiritual Nature of Man* by A Hardy, 1979, by permission of Oxford University Press; Perseus Books Group for extracts from *Same Sex Different Cultures* by G Herdt, 1997; SPCK for the extract from *Science and Creation* by J Polkinghorne; © Space Time Publications 1988. Extracted from *A brief History of Time* published by Bantam Press, a division of Transworld Publishers Ltd; From *Same Sex Different Cultures* by Gilbert Herdt. Copyright © 1997 by Westview Press; *The Bhagavad Gita* translated by Juan Mascaró, 1962, reproduced by permission of Penguin Books Ltd; *The Upanishads* translated by Juan Mascaró, 1965, reproduced by permission of Penguin Books Ltd; Quotations from the English translation of the Catechism of the Catholic Church for Australia © 1994 St Pauls, Strathfield, Australia/Libreria Editrice Vaticana used with permission. All rights reserved.

Scriptures quoted from The Holy Bible, New International Version by Hodder & Stoughton © 1973, 1978, 1984 International Bible Society, with permission; The Holy Qur'an, translated by Yusuf Ali © IPCI, with permission.

The publishers would like to thank the following individuals, institutions and companies for permission to reproduce photographs and illustrations in this book:

AKG Photo London/Andre Normil, 'Die Arch Noah', p150; Anglican World p132; Associated Press AP p72, 122, 129; © BBC p93, 94, 95, 97; Camerapress (Theodore Wood) p17, (Ian Lloyd) p23; Christine Osborne Pictures p44; Circa Photo Library p56, (Zbignieu Kosc) p12, (William Holtby) p14, 56, 74, (Barrie Searle) p28, 37, (Robyn Beeche) p30, (John Fryer) p32, (Ged Murray) p36, (John Smith) p43; Seamus Conlon/Fotora du Monde p109; Corbis (David H Wells) p53, (Michael St. Maur Sheil) p73, (David N Wells) p53, (Catherine Karnov) p69, (Stephanie Maze) p84, (Mitch Gerber) p136, (Kevin Schafer) p149; M I El-Dessouki p25, 26; Philip Emmett p58, 62, 142; Eye Ubiquitous/Trip 10; Format (Paula Solloway) p48, (Jenny Matthews) p49; Ian Jones/FSP/Gamma p60; Health Education Authority p138; The Hutchinson Library (B Régent) p48; Jewish AIDS Trust p141; The Jewish National Fund p120; Knock, Our Lady's Shrine p66; Life File (Andrew Ward) p47, 77, (Arthur Jumper) p105, (Tim Fisher) p106; Lfi-UFB/Freddy Baez p19; Mirror Syndication International p88; Muslim Aid p101; Network (Mike Goldwater) p51; Oxford Designers & Illustrators p68; "PA" News p89, (Brian Little) p125; Pitkin Unichrome Ltd p57, 78; Reverend Dr J C Polkinghorne p151; David Rose p8, 45; Science Photo Library (Mehau Kulyk) p67, (David A. Hardy) 148; Still Pictures (Carlos Guarita/Reportage) p100, (Elaine Duigenan) 107; Superstock Inc. (Xavier Jones) p70; Swaminarayan Mandir, Neasden p39, 46, 82, 103; Mel Thompson p31, 46; World Jewish Relief p102.

Every effort has been made to trace and acknowledge copyright. The publishers will be happy to make suitable arrangements with any copyright holder whom it has not been possible to contact.

For Benjamin and Kisa

The author would like to express his grateful thanks to the following:

Jill Watton for her support and encouragement, and excellent photography; Chris Metcalfe and the pupils of Bishopsgarth School, Stockton-on-Tees, and the staff and pupils of the Ian Ramsey School for their help in testing materials; Yasmeen Amehd and family, and Muhammed El-Dessouki for their help with Muslim illustrations; Steve Bowler and John Rudge for support from London Exams; Sadhu Atmaswarupdas and the Swaminaryan Mandir, Neasden for their assistance with illustrations and quotes from His Holiness Pramukh Swami Maharaj (BAPS); Jeffery Blumenfeld at the Jewish Marriage Counsel, the Office of the Chief Rabbi and Rabbi Julian Jacobs for their help on Jewish moral attitudes.

Orders: please contact Bookpoint Ltd, 39 Milton Park, Abingdon, Oxon OX14 4TD. Telephone: (44) 01235 400414, Fax: (44) 01235 400454. Lines are open from 9.00–6.00, Monday to Saturday, with a 24 hour message answering service. Email address: orders@bookpoint.co.uk

British Library Cataloguing in Publication Data
A catalogue record for this title is available from The British Library

ISBN 0 340 74305 0

First published 1999
Impression number   10 9 8 7 6 5 4 3
Year   2004 2003 2002 2001 2000

Cover photo from Images.
Typeset by Wearset, Boldon, Tyne and Wear.
Printed in Dubai for Hodder & Stoughton Educational, a division of Hodder Headline Plc, 338 Euston Road, London NW1 3BH by Oriental Press .

CONTENTS

Preface   6

Introduction   7

Chapter 1 Marriage and the Family   16

Factfile 1   Social facts on marriage, divorce and family life   16
Factfile 2   Christian teaching on marriage and divorce   20
Factfile 3   Muslim teaching on marriage and divorce   24
Factfile 4   Jewish teaching on marriage and divorce   27
Factfile 5   Hindu teaching on marriage and divorce   30
Factfile 6   Christianity and the family   32
Factfile 7   Islam and the family   34
Factfile 8   Judaism and the family   36
Factfile 9   Hinduism and the family   38
Questions   40

Chapter 2 Social Harmony   41

Factfile 10   Social facts concerning the roles of men and
              women   41
Factfile 11   Christianity and the roles of men and
              women   42
Factfile 12   Islam and the roles of men and women   44
Factfile 13   Judaism and the roles of men and women   45
Factfile 14   Hinduism and the roles of men and women   46
Factfile 15   Social facts concerning the UK as a
              multi-ethnic society   47
Factfile 16   Christianity and racial harmony   50
Factfile 17   Islam and racial harmony   52
Factfile 18   Judaism and racial harmony   53
Factfile 19   Hinduism and racial harmony   54
Factfile 20   Britain as a multi-faith society   54
Factfile 21   Christianity and other religions   57
Factfile 22   Islam and other religions   58
Factfile 23   Judaism and other religions   59
Factfile 24   Hinduism and other religions   59
Factfile 25   Religions working together   60
Questions   61

Chapter 3 Believing in God   62

Factfile 26   Religious upbringing and belief in God   62
Factfile 27   Religious experience and belief in God   64
Factfile 28   Experience of the world and belief in God   67
Factfile 29   The problem of evil and suffering   69
Factfile 30   Christian responses to evil and suffering   70
Factfile 31   Islamic responses to evil and suffering   72
Factfile 32   Jewish responses to evil and suffering   72
Factfile 33   Hindu responses to evil and suffering   74
Questions   75

Chapter 4 Issues of Life and Death   76

Factfile 34 The sanctity of life   76
Factfile 35 Christian teaching on life after death   78
Factfile 36 Muslim teaching on life after death   80
Factfile 37 Jewish teaching on life after death   81
Factfile 38 Hindu teaching on life after death   82
Factfile 39 Social facts on abortion   83
Factfile 40 Christianity and abortion   84
Factfile 41 Islam and abortion   85
Factfile 42 Judaism and abortion   86
Factfile 43 Hinduism and abortion   86
Factfile 44 Social facts on euthanasia   87
Factfile 45 Christianity and euthanasia   89
Factfile 46 Islam and euthanasia   90
Factfile 47 Judaism and euthanasia   90
Factfile 48 Hinduism and euthanasia   90
Questions   91

Chapter 5 Religion and the Media   92

Factfile 49 Introduction   92
Factfile 50 Worship and magazine programmes   94
Factfile 51 Religious documentaries   95
Factfile 52 Religious and moral issues in soaps and drama 96
Questions   98

Chapter 6 Religion, Wealth and Poverty   99

Factfile 53 Christian teaching on wealth and poverty   99
Factfile 54 Muslim teaching on wealth and poverty   101
Factfile 55 Jewish teaching on wealth and poverty   102
Factfile 56 Hindu teaching on wealth and poverty   103
Factfile 57 The need for world development   104
Factfile 58 The work of Christian organisations to relieve poverty   106
Questions   110

Chapter 7 Religion and the Environment   111

Factfile 59 Environmental issues   111
Factfile 60 Christianity and the environment   114
Factfile 61 Islam and the environment   115
Factfile 62 Judaism and the environment   117
Factfile 63 Hinduism and the environment   119
Factfile 64 The Jewish National Fund and the environment   120
Questions   121

Chapter 8 Peace and War   122

Factfile 65 War and peace issues   122
Factfile 66 Christianity and war   123
Factfile 67 Islam and war   126
Factfile 68 Judaism and war   127
Factfile 69 Hinduism and war   128
Questions   130

Chapter 9 Religion and Homosexuality   131

Factfile 70 The social background   131
Factfile 71 Christianity and homosexuality   132
Factfile 72 Islam and homosexuality   134
Factfile 73 Judaism and homosexuality   135
Factfile 74 Hinduism and homosexuality   136
Questions   137

Chapter 10 Religion and Medical Issues   138

Factfile 75 Contraception   138
Factfile 76 Christianity and contraception   139
Factfile 77 Islam and contraception   140
Factfile 78 Judaism and contraception   141
Factfile 79 Hinduism and contraception   142
Factfile 80 Religion and infertility   143
Questions   146

Chapter 11 Religion and Science   147

Factfile 81 How science and religion are connected   147
Factfile 82 Science and creation   149
Questions   152

Useful Addresses   153

How Religion and Life Covers the Short Courses   154

Index   155

PREFACE

This book has been revised in the light of teachers' comments, and the experience of the examinations over the past two years, to give a better preparation for the GCSE short courses in Religious Education.

The addition of five new chapters means that it now covers almost all of the issues examined by NEAB, MEG, SEG and the Welsh Board.

In conjunction with the *Teacher's Handbook*, it provides a complete resource for those preparing for any of the five Religion and Life units set at GCSE by London Examinations.

It provides resources on Christianity, Islam, Hinduism, and Judaism which are in 'factfiles' colour coded by religion. Those wishing to study Buddhism or Sikhism alongside Christianity will find it helpful to use *Buddhism – a New Approach* or *Sikhism – A New Approach* in conjunction with this book. These are also published by Hodder and Stoughton.

There is no criticism of the religious attitudes covered in this book. This is to encourage students to think and evaluate for themselves. However, the *Teacher's Handbook* has photocopiable sheets of alternative viewpoints and revision files of each topic in the London syllabuses.

When dates are given in the non-Christian religions, the letters CE and BCE are used. These stand for Common Era and Before the Common Era, as AD and BC imply belief in Christianity.

I hope that students and teachers will find this revised edition even more useful and enjoyable than the first edition.

INTRODUCTION

Most of you will have studied Christianity, and probably the other religion you are offering for GCSE, up to Key Stage 3, but here is a reminder of some background facts about these religions which will be essential for your GCSE course:

CHRISTIANITY

Basic Christian beliefs

- Christians believe that there is only one God, who acts in the world as Father, Son and Holy Spirit (the TRINITY).

- They believe that God created the world and humans in his image. God is love, and out of love, he sent his son to live and die for humanity.

- Many Christians believe that Jesus died to save people from the punishment which human sin deserves – death. They believe that if people believe in Jesus as God's son and their saviour, they will have eternal life in heaven.

- Christians believe that the Bible is the word of God. Although they have different opinions about exactly what this means, they all believe that the Bible tells the truth about Jesus and contains the Christian teachings about God and how life should be lived.

How Christians make moral decisions

- All Christians believe that moral decisions should be based on the teachings of Jesus in the New Testament and the Ten Commandments in the Old Testament.

- ROMAN CATHOLICS believe that these teachings are best interpreted by the Church, especially the Head of the Church – the Pope. So, to make moral decisions, they would refer to the teachings of the Church contained in *The Catechism of the Catholic Church* (1994) or Encyclicals (long letters containing the Pope's teachings) published by the Pope.

- ORTHODOX CHRISTIANS would base their decisions on how the Bible has been interpreted by councils of bishops, or simply ask advice from their priest (many Catholics would also do this).

- PROTESTANTS (Church of England, Methodist, Baptist, Pentecostal etc.) believe that each individual should make their own decision on the basis of what the Bible says, but most would also be guided by decisions made by

Factfiles concerning Christian beliefs and ideas are colour coded like this:

democratically elected bodies of Church leaders (e.g. the General Synod of the Church of England or the Conference of the Methodist Church).

Why there may be differences of opinion among Christians

- Christianity developed in different places in different ways. By the time Christianity became the official religion of the Roman Empire in 356 CE, there were several different traditions within Christianity. In the West, the Bishop of Rome (the Pope) became accepted as leader among the bishops in that part of the Empire. The Eastern Churches (Orthodox) were ruled by councils of bishops. By 1054, the Eastern and Western branches of the Church had divided from one another.

- In the sixteenth century, men like Martin Luther and John Calvin accused the Western Church of going a long way from the Church of the New Testament. They protested and demanded reforms (the Reformation). This led to the Protestant or Reformed Churches which believed in the Church being ruled democratically (they taught that all Christian believers are priests and therefore equal with each other) and in the absolute authority of the Bible.

  More recently, some Protestant Christians decided that there was too much interpretation of the Bible without accepting the Bible as the absolute word of God. These Evangelical Christians emphasise the need for conversion (being born again by accepting Jesus Christ as your saviour) and for accepting the Bible as the words of God. They are sometimes known as fundamentalists because they want to go back to the fundamentals (basics) of the Christian religion.

  All Christian Churches have also been influenced by the Charismatic Movement which emphasises the need for Christians to be filled with the Holy Spirit and consult God directly, through the Holy Spirit, when needing advice. Charismatic Christians practise spiritual healing and speaking in tongues.

- Differences of opinion among Christians may therefore arise because of:
  - the way they understand the authority of the Church;
  - the way they interpret the Bible;
  - the importance they place on the Holy Spirit;
  - the importance they place on their own personal experience.

Examples:

Orthodox, Roman Catholic and some Evangelicals do not allow women priests, other Christians do.

Roman Catholics do not allow contraception, other Christians do.

Charismatics and many Evangelicals believe it is right to try to convert members of other religions, other Christians do not.

Catholic and Evangelical Christians believe homosexuality is condemned by God, other Christians do not.

Shared ministry is one way Churches are coming together.

ISLAM

Muslims always refer to God as Allah because this is the Arabic word used for God in the Qur'an. However, in this book, the word God is used so that non-Muslims do not think Muslims are worshipping a different god.

Basic Muslim beliefs

- Islam means submission to God's will which brings peace to the world. Muslims believe it was the original religion given by God to Adam, the first man and first prophet.

- Muslims believe there is only one God who made the world and humans to act in unity with him and with each other. God's oneness is so important that the worst sin for a Muslim is to associate other beings or things with God (so Muslims cannot worship pop stars or football heroes).

- Muslims believe that Muhammad was given God's absolute and final word (the QUR'AN), directly by God and that, because it was written down immediately in the way God wanted, there will never be a need for another prophet.

- Muhammad established Islam not only as a religion, but also as a community (ummah) with all its laws based on the teachings of the Qur'an.

- Muslims believe that the purpose of life is to worship God. They follow God's laws as God revealed them to Muhammad and practise the five Pillars of belief, prayer, giving to the poor, fasting in Ramadan and going on pilgrimage to Mecca (Makkah). If all this is done, then, after death, they will go to heaven for eternity.

Factfiles concerning Muslim beliefs and ideas are colour coded like this:

How Muslims make moral decisions

- Because Islam began as a community religion, there has always been an Islamic legal system based on God's laws. This is known as the SHARI'AH (the way God wants men to walk). The Shari'ah is based mainly on God's words in the Qur'an, though it also uses the Sunnah (examples and sayings of Muhammad as recorded in hadith). Muslims believe that Muhammad was the final prophet sent by God and so what Muhammad said and did is the final example for humans on how to live their lives.

- So when Muslims make moral decisions, they find out what the Shari'ah says. If this does not cover the particular point, then they will ask a Muslim lawyer for advice (Muslim lawyers are also religious leaders) or read the Qur'an to see if that gives a relevant teaching.

- Everything Muslims are allowed to do is called HALAL and everything they are forbidden to do is called HARAM.

Some Muslim Law Schools say eating shellfish is wrong, others say it is allowed.

Shi'ah Muslims allow men to have a temporary marriage, Sunnis do not.

Some Muslims say it is wrong to watch TV programmes showing the sexes mixing and women in non-islamic clothes, others say it is all right as long as they are not doing evil things.

Some Muslims are trying to restore a Muslim empire, others think Muslims should have their own countries like Pakistan and Egypt.

Why there may be differences of opinion among Muslims

- When the Shari'ah was being sorted out, there were some differences of opinion between Muslim scholars and four law schools were established (Hanifite, Hanbalite, Malikite, Shafi'ite) and Muslim lawyers belong to one of these schools. Each Muslim country follows the Shari'ah as set down by one of these schools and so there are bound to be some differences.

- Most Muslims (85 per cent) are Sunni (follow only the sunnah of Muhammad). However, some are Shi'ah who also follow the hadith of Ali (Muhammad's cousin and son-in-law) and the teachings of Muhammad's descendants through Ali. The Shi'ah are therefore bound to have some differences of opinion from the Sunni.

- The Shari'ah dates to the Prophet Muhammad but was not formalised until 900 CE, so it has no rulings on things like TV. Lawyers have to work out laws on these, and lawyers can disagree.

- Some Muslims think there should be one state of Islam joining all Muslim countries together. Others think there should be separate Muslim countries like Pakistan and Saudi Arabia.

The Holy Ka'aba, the centre of Islam.

JUDAISM

Jews always refer to God as, The Almighty, because they think God's name is too holy to be used. However, in this book, the word God is used so that non-Jews do not think Jews are worshipping a different god.

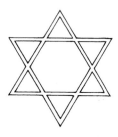

Basic Jewish beliefs

- Jews believe that there is only one God who is righteous and good and who is to be worshipped by following his moral commands (ETHICAL MONOTHEISM).

- They believe that God created the world and humans. They believe that God chose people like Adam and Noah to tell the world about him and to keep true religion. Then God chose Abraham and made a special COVENANT with Abraham that he would give Abraham and his descendants the land of Canaan and make a great nation of his descendants as long as Abraham and his descendants kept God's laws.

- They believe that God made a covenant with the Jews through Abraham and Moses. As part of the covenant made with Moses, God gave the Torah, God's commandments, so that by following it, the Jews could be God's holy nation and bring the rest of the world to true worship of God.

- Jews believe that if they try to keep all God's commandments, then their names will be recorded in the book of life.

- Their holy book is called the TENAKH (the same as the Protestant Christian Old Testament). It is in three parts: TORAH (the 'laws' given to Moses), NEVIIM (the 'prophets' including the historical writings) and KETUVIM (the 'writings' e.g. Psalms).

Factfiles concerning Jewish beliefs and ideas are colour coded like this:

How Jews make moral decisions

- Jews believe that there are commandments of God (MITZVOT) for every situation in life. These are found in the Torah and are explained in the TALMUD, a collection of Jewish teachings which dates from about 500 CE.

- Where it is difficult to decide what these mitzvot mean for today, Jews rely on rabbis who are expert in the Torah and Talmud, and on the decisions of great rabbis in the past. These decisions form the basis of detailed guidelines for how to live your life as a Jew and are called HALAKHAH (path).

- Every country with a sizeable Jewish population has a Bet Din made up of the best qualified and most respected rabbis who make decisions for the Jews of their country on new moral issues and on matters like divorce.

- Jews are therefore totally dependent on God's commandments for making moral decisions.

Why there may be differences of opinion among Jews

Examples:

Some Jews (mainly Hasidic) believe Israel should not have been founded until the Messiah arrived.

Reform, Liberal and many Orthodox Jews believe you can wear whatever clothes you like, as long as men cover their heads, but the Hasidic and some Orthodox believe Jews must wear special clothes.

Reform and Liberal Jews give men and women equal divorce rights; Orthodox and Hasidic only allow divorce if the husband agrees.

Reform and Liberal Jews allow women to sit with men in the synagogues, Orthodox and Hasidic do not.

- For nearly two thousand years there was no homeland or centre for Judaism, so different interpretations arose in different areas. In particular the Jews living in the Muslim Empire (now called Sephardi Jews) and those living in Europe (called Ashkenazi Jews) developed different interpretations and even developed different popular forms of the Hebrew language.

- In the seventeenth and eighteenth centuries there was argument among European Jews about the need for joy and closeness to God. Hasidic Judaism developed from this debate.

- In the nineteenth century there were calls to modernise Judaism. The Orthodox (who include Sephardi, Ashkenazi and Hasidic Jews) said Jews had to obey all God's commands literally, but two new groups, Reform Jews and Liberal Jews, said that the Law needed to be interpreted, so that Judaism could adapt to the needs of the modern world.

Orthodox Jews praying at the Western Wall of the Temple of Jerusalem.

HINDUISM

Basic Hindu Beliefs

- The name Hinduism is a word used by Westerners to refer to the native religions of India, but it is better to speak of Hinduisms because there is no one religion with a set of clear beliefs.

- There are many different forms of Hinduism. Some Hindus worship several gods, some worship only one. Generally Hindus tend to believe that there is a universal soul (Brahman) which is revealed in the various gods and goddesses of Hinduism and in the soul of every living creature.

- Hindus regard the Vedas, Upanishads, Gita and Ramayana as holy books, but they do not think of them in the same way that Jews, Muslims or Christians think of their scriptures. Hindus are guided by them, but do not think of them as the word of God.

- Hindus believe that life is like a wheel – you are born, you live, you die, you are re-born (reincarnation). Life is governed by the law of cause and effect (KARMA) and the purpose of life is to achieve liberation (MOKSHA) from the wheel of life and the law of karma.

- What you are re-born as depends on your actions. Everyone is set a path of actions (DHARMA) which, if fulfilled, will lead to salvation.

- The ideas of karma and dharma have influenced the caste system where what you are born as is determined by your previous existence and you must do your dharma in that caste if you are to achieve salvation.

Factfiles concerning Hindu beliefs and ideas are colour coded like this:

How Hindus make moral decisions

- Tradition lays down what is the dharma for each caste. Every Hindu is supposed to follow four stages of life (ashramas). The first of these is the student ashrama, when Hindu children are taught the dharma for their caste. These traditions are taught and/or interpreted by brahmins (priests) and are based on Hindu law codes such as the Code of Manu (they are not based on the scriptures).

- When new situations arise, Hindus tend to rely on the teachings of the gurus or swamis (teachers or spiritual leaders) who lead their Hindu sect.

- Some Hindus act as their own guru and make moral decisions based on what they think Hinduism is.

- There are bound to be different practices in Hinduism, because there are so many different forms of Hinduism and new groups are appearing all the time. For example, the temple in Neasden is the work of the Swaminarayan Hindu Mission. Other Hindu sects in Britain include Hare Krishna (Iskcon), Sai Baba and Rama Krishna Vedenta Mission.

Dedicated to God at Varanasi on the holy River Ganges.

Examples:

Some Hindus are vegetarian, others eat meat (but not beef).

Some Hindus refuse to drink alcohol, others believe it is a gift from God.

Some Hindus believe in the caste system, others (like the Swaminarayan) have rejected the caste system.

Some Hindus think you ought to marry to fulfil your householder ashrama, others think you can by-pass this stage and dedicate yourself to God instead of marrying.

Differences and similarities between religions

Although there are differences within and between religions, the differences can be exaggerated. As can be seen in the issues covered in this book, some Christians, Muslims, Jews and Hindus agree more with each other on an issue than with fellow members of their own religion.

Not all members of a religion have the same ideas. An Orthodox Jew may refuse to use a car to go to synagogue, but have liberal attitudes on the status of women. A Catholic Christian may attend a Catholic church, but have Protestant views on contraception.

People are individuals and so, although general statements can be made about the beliefs and attitudes of a religion, there will always be individual members of the religion who do not fit the statement.

NON-RELIGIOUS PEOPLE AND MORAL ISSUES

It is often thought that people need religion to behave in a moral way, but non-religious people can be very moral people, just as some religious people can be immoral.

Non-religious people use one or more of the following ideas when making moral decisions:

- Some look at what the law says. For example, if they were thinking about whether to give euthanasia to someone they loved, they would look at the law and not use euthanasia because the law bans it.

- Some look at the consequences of an action. They ask themselves what the results would be of the different choices they could make. Often they are guided by which result will bring the greatest happiness or the least misery to the most people (this is known in philosophy as Utilitarianism). For example, if looking at the issue of abortion, they would look to see whether banning abortions would bring greater happiness and less misery than allowing them. If they thought it would, they would not have an abortion.

- Some use the idea that because people have to live with each other in the world, they should use their instinct to guide them to what is right and then work out what it would be like if everyone did what their instinct is telling them. For example, if their instinct told them it was right to have an abortion, they would then work out what the world would be like if everyone in their situation had an abortion. If they decided it would make the world a better place, then they would have the abortion.

LABOUR'S NEW SLEAZE
BOTH RELIGIOUS AND NON-RELIGIOUS PEOPLE ARGUE ABOUT THE MORALITY OF POLITICIANS

1 MARRIAGE AND THE FAMILY

SOCIAL FACTS ON MARRIAGE, DIVORCE AND FAMILY LIFE

MARRIAGE – THE CONDITION OF A MAN AND WOMAN LEGALLY UNITED FOR THE PURPOSE OF LIVING TOGETHER, AND, USUALLY, CREATING LAWFUL OFFSPRING.

DIVORCE – LEGALLY DISSOLVE A MARRIAGE SO THAT THE PARTNERS ARE FREE TO MARRY SOMEONE ELSE.

COHABITATION – A MAN AND WOMAN LIVING TOGETHER WITHOUT BEING MARRIED.

PROMISCUITY – HAVING SEXUAL INTERCOURSE WITH SEVERAL PARTNERS AND WITHOUT COMMITMENT. IT IS OFTEN CALLED 'CASUAL SEX'. IN THE BIBLE THIS IS OFTEN CALLED FORNICATION.

ADULTERY – AN ACT OF SEXUAL INTERCOURSE BETWEEN A MARRIED PERSON AND SOMEONE OTHER THAN THEIR MARRIAGE PARTNER.

MONOGAMY – MARRIAGE TO ONE PARTNER ONLY.

POLYGAMY – MARRIAGE TO MORE THAN ONE PARTNER AT A TIME.

SERIAL MONOGAMY – MARRYING ONLY ONE PARTNER AT A TIME, BUT DIVORCING AND REMARRYING SEVERAL TIMES.

NUCLEAR FAMILY – MOTHER, FATHER AND CHILDREN LIVING AS A UNIT.

EXTENDED FAMILY – GRANDPARENTS/AUNTS/UNCLES LIVING AS A UNIT (OR LIVING VERY CLOSE AND HAVING A LOT OF CONTACT).

ONE-PARENT FAMILY – WHERE ONLY ONE OF THE PARENTS IS BRINGING UP THE CHILDREN (THIS CAN BE BECAUSE OF SEPARATION, DIVORCE, DEATH OF MARRIAGE PARTNER OR UNMARRIED PARENT)

RECONSTITUTED FAMILY – WHERE TWO SETS OF CHILDREN (STEP-BROTHERS AND SISTERS) BECOME ONE FAMILY WHEN THEIR DIVORCED PARENTS MARRY EACH OTHER.

TABLE 1 Marriage 1971-1995 England and Wales

	1971	1989	1993	1995
Number of marriages (thousands)	405	347	299	292
Number of couples cohabiting rather than marrying	–	18%	–	25%

Source: Social Trends 28.

Many people, not just the famous, have chosen to cohabit rather than to marry.

Fifty per cent of all marriages take place in Church. Many people marry without a religious ceremony as 50 per cent of marriages take place in registry offices. These are known as civil marriages and require the couple to make vows promising to stay with each other for life. Since 1995 such marriages do not have to take place in a registry office; people can now marry on the beach, in a park etc. as long as that place is registered.

TABLE 2 Changes in the divorce law of the UK

	YEAR
Divorce only allowed by Act of Parliament	1534
Civil divorce allowed on grounds of adultery only	1857
Desertion, cruelty and insanity allowed as grounds for divorce	1937
Irretrievable breakdown allowed as grounds for divorce and cheaper divorce introduced	1969

TABLE 3 Divorce 1961-1996 England and Wales

	1961	1971	1981	1991	1993	1996
Number of divorces (thousands)	25	74	146	151	165	155
Divorce rate (divorces per 1000 population)	2.1	5.9	11.9	12.7	–	13.5
Children (aged under 16) of divorcing couples (thousands)	35*	82	159	148	176	161

* = all children no statistics for under 16's

Source: Social Trends 28.

Statements on divorce from a newspaper article.

My parents are getting divorced

My parents are in their 50s and divorcing (20 years too late, I think). I love them both, but they want me to take sides. Where do I turn?

I can't forget him

I'm an Asian woman of 28. I've been married for 10 years and have four children. I've had my fair share of problems with my husband, but we're very happy now.

A while ago I had a fling with a 20-year-old guy. We never made love, just shared special moments together. But it got to the stage where it affected my life. I was in love with him but I could do nothing except end the whole thing. As Asians we are brought up in a very strict culture and it is a disgrace to leave our family.

I still love this guy and can't forget him, yet I love my husband as well. It's driving me crazy.

Problem pages are full of letters about the problems of relationships, adultery and divorce.

The charity One plus One published a report claiming to show that married people live longer, have healthier lives, suffer less stress and mental illness and are financially better off than the single, divorced or widowed. Fiona McAllister, the researcher who wrote the charity's report, drew on evidence from across Europe and the United States to demonstrate the link between marital breakdown and physical and mental ill-health... Data from the Office of Population Censuses and Surveys, she claimed, showed that divorced men aged 45–49 had a 76 per cent extra risk of premature death compared with those in marriages. For women of the same age, she found a 39 per cent extra risk.

Ms McAllister concedes that it may be that better balanced and healthier people are more likely to marry and stay wed, but believes the main reason for marriage's protective effect is that the institution provides support against stress and anxiety.

Doctor Patrick Dixon author of a book, *The Rising Price of Love*, said divorce would also have long-term effects on children in the families concerned, 'Divorce often means poor exam results, damaged health and stress, four times the risk of needing psychiatric help as a child and a greater risk of breakdown in middle age.'

TABLE 4 BIRTHS OUTSIDE MARRIAGE

	1971	1977	1981	1989	1993	1996
Percentage of births	8	10	13	27	32	35
Percentage of joint registrations (likely to indicate parents living together)	46	–	–	71	75	80

Source: Social Trends 28.

TABLE 5 FAMILIES WITH DEPENDENT CHILDREN

Family Type	1971	1975	1981	1989
2 parent	92%	90%	87%	81%
Single mother	1%	1%	2%	6%
Divorced/separated mother	4%	5%	6%	11%
Widowed mother	2%	2%	2%	1%
Lone father	1%	1%	2%	2%

Source: Social Trends 28.

TABLE 6 THESE RESPONSES TO A 1997 QUESTIONNAIRE SHOW THE FAMILY IS NOT DYING

People should keep in touch with close family members even if they have little in common	70% agreed
People should keep in touch with relatives such as aunts, uncles, cousins even though they have little in common	56% agreed
People should always turn to their family before asking the state for help	48% agreed
Children should still expect help from their parents even when they have left home	88% agreed

Source: Social Trends 28.

In September 1998 the BBC and Disney spent two million pounds on 13 half hour episodes of *Microsoap* which they billed as the first children's programme to tackle divorce from the viewpoint of the children. The producers claimed that usual children's programmes are out of touch with the reality of children's lives because they show normal families as having a happily married Mum and Dad whereas a large proportion of children now come from broken homes.

Microsoap featured the lives of nine-year-old Joe and twelve-year-old Emily not only coming to terms with their mother and father splitting up but also with their mother's boyfriend whose children have a totally different lifestyle.

Does the fact that children's television now makes comedies for children out of divorce and reconstituted families mean that the family is disappearing, or is a family something different from mother, father and children?

Madonna is bringing up her baby as a single mother.

CHRISTIAN TEACHING ON MARRIAGE AND DIVORCE

Introduction

All Christians agree that sex should be restricted to marriage and that marriage should be for life. They regard adultery as a sin. They do not teach that everyone should marry. It is up to the individual to decide what God wants them to do with their life. There are some differences among Christians about whether marriage is a sacrament (Roman Catholics, Orthodox and Church of England believe it is) and whether divorce is allowable (all Churches except the Roman Catholic believe it is, but have rules about re-marriage).

In most Churches it is necessary for both bride and groom to be Christians and in some they must belong to the same denomination.

Many brides marry in white as a sign of purity, but this is not a religious requirement. Christian marriages usually end with a wedding party.

> But among you there must not even be a hint of sexual immorality or of any kind of impurity.

Ephesians 5:3

> You shall not commit adultery.

Exodus 20:14

> The sexual act must take place exclusively within marriage. Outside marriage it always constitutes a grave sin and excludes one from sacramental communion.

Catechism of the Catholic Church.

Christian Attitudes to Sex outside Marriage

All Christians believe that promiscuity is wrong. There are many verses in the Bible which say that sexual immorality (promiscuity/fornication) is sinful and must be avoided by Christians. All Christian Churches have made statements condemning promiscuity.

Most Christians believe that sex before marriage is wrong and this includes cohabitation. Most Christians believe that living as husband and wife without being married is 'living in sin'.

There are, however, some differences among Christians about cohabitation. Some liberal Protestants now accept that couples may want to live together before marrying and do not condemn them for this. However, they would expect them to marry when starting a family and would not approve of casual relationships. A report published by the Church of England's Board of Responsibility in 1995, *Something to Celebrate*, said that cohabiting couples should be welcomed and supported by the Church, 'recognising that for many this is a step along the way to the fuller commitment of marriage'. There have been similar reports by the Methodist Church and the Society of Friends (Quakers).

All Christians regard adultery as a great sin. Not only is it condemned in the Ten Commandments, but in all Christian wedding ceremonies, couples promise that they will only have sex with each other. So, if they have sex with someone other than their marriage partner, they are breaking their marriage vows, the promises they made to God.

Carey speaks out on 'living in sin'

A provisional, purely private arrangement is not as good a framework as marriage for the nurture of families.

Christian Attitudes to marriage

All Christians agree that sex should be restricted to marriage, but there is no requirement for Christians to marry. It is up to an individual person to decide what they feel God wants them to do with their life. If they feel God wants them to share their life with someone, then they should marry.

All Christians believe that marriage is intended as a lifelong union.

The Roman Catholic Church, the Orthodox Church and the Church of England believe that marriage is a sacrament. Sacraments are public actions by which Christians receive grace, that is, experience the power and love of God in their lives. These Churches believe that the marriage ceremony gives the couple the grace of God to help make their marriage work. Other Churches do not regard marriage as a sacrament, but feel the grace comes from the prayers.

In most Churches, it is necessary for both bride and groom to be Christians, but those Churches which do not regard marriage as sacrament may arrange a special service for a mixed faith wedding. In some Churches, both bride and groom must belong to the same Church for a full wedding ceremony to take place.

Marriage in Church does not have to be conventional...

Marriage is given, that husband and wife may comfort and help each other, living faithfully together in need and in plenty, in sorrow and in joy. It is given, that with delight and tenderness they may know each other in love and, through the joy of their bodily union, may strengthen the union of their hearts and lives. It is given that they may have children and be blessed in caring for them and bringing them up in accordance with God's will.

Church of England Alternative Service Book.

Are you ready freely and without reservation to give yourselves to each other in marriage? Are your ready to love and honour each other as man and wife for the rest of your lives? Are you ready to accept children lovingly from God, and bring them up according to the law of Christ and his Church?

Roman Catholic Rite of Marriage During Mass.

I, N, take you, N, to be my husband, to have and to hold from this day forward; for better, for worse, for richer, for poorer, in sickness and in health, to love and to cherish, till death us do part, according to God's holy law; and this is my solemn vow.

Church of England Alternative Service Book.

> In the presence of God, and before this congregation, N and N have given their consent and made their marriage vows to each other. They have declared their marriage by the joining of hands and the giving and receiving of a ring. I therefore proclaim that they are husband and wife. That which God has joined together, let not man divide.

Church of England Alternative Service Book.

The purpose of Christian marriage

Christians believe that marriage is a gift from God which was given:

a) for a woman and a man to share love and companionship;
b) for a man and a woman to enjoy sex with each other in the way God wants;
c) so that children can be brought into the world;
d) so that children can be brought up in a Christian family and become members of Christ's Church;
e) as a way for a woman and a man to show their love for each other and to gain God's grace to help them in their married life.

The main features of a Christian marriage service are:

1 Talk and Bible readings on the nature of Christian marriage;
2 The exchange of vows committing the partners to a lifetime of Christian marriage and restricting sex to each other;
3 The exchange of rings symbolising the unending nature of marriage;
4 Prayers asking God's blessing on the couple and the help of the Holy Spirit to make the marriage work;
5 Emphasis that God is part of a marriage and that this makes it for life.

Christian Teachings on Divorce

> **But at the beginning of creation God 'made them male and female'. For this reason a man will leave his father and mother and be united with his wife and the two will become one flesh. So they are no longer two, but one. Therefore what God has joined together, let man not separate.**

Mark 10:6–9

There are major disagreements among Christians about divorce and remarriage.

Almost all Christians disapprove of divorce as they believe that the marriage vows made before God require a couple to stay together until they are parted by death.

Most Protestant and Orthodox Churches allow divorce and remarriage. These Christians claim that Jesus allowed divorce in Matthew 19:9 and that, as Christianity is about the forgiveness of sins, if people repent of their mistakes, they should be allowed another chance. Often these Churches require divorced people wanting to remarry to have special preparation and to demonstrate clearly that they repent of their mistakes and are determined to make their second marriage last for life.

The Roman Catholic Church does not allow divorce. Marriage is a sacrament and the exchange of vows means that the only way a marriage can be dissolved (this is what divorce means) is by death. Jesus said in Mark 10:10–12 that if people divorce and remarry, they are committing adultery, so divorce cannot be permitted.

However, the Roman Catholic Church does allow the annulment of a marriage. This is different from divorce because divorce dissolves a marriage, whereas annulment says that the marriage was not a proper marriage and so it never existed in the eyes of God. Annulments are granted if:
a) one of the partners was not baptised at the time of the marriage;
b) one of the partners was forced into the marriage;
c) one of the partners did not intend to keep the marriage vows at the time of making them;
d) one of the partners was mentally unstable at the time of the marriage.

The Church of England disapproves of divorce, but accepts that it may be the lesser of two evils in certain cases. It leaves it up to individual priests to decide whether to remarry divorced couples.

... but it can be very formal.

For those who have taken their vows before God as Christians, there is no divorce. But most Baptists would acknowledge that human beings can make mistakes and what appeared at the time as a life-long relationship may eventually break down. In this case would it not be better to confess failure and in true repentance acknowledge their guilt and ask for forgiveness?

Statement of the Baptist Church in *What the Churches Say on Moral Issues.*

When they were in the house again, the disciples asked Jesus about this. He answered, 'Anyone who divorces his wife and marries another woman commits adultery against her. And if she divorces her husband and marries another man, she commits adultery.'

Mark 10:10-12

Jesus replied, 'Moses permitted you to divorce your wives because your hearts were hard. But it was not this way from the beginning. I tell you that anyone who divorces his wife, except for marital unfaithfulness, and marries another woman commits adultery.'

Matthew 19:8–9

Between the baptised, a ratified and consummated marriage cannot be dissolved by any human power or for any reason other than death.

Catechism of the Catholic Church.

MUSLIM TEACHING ON MARRIAGE AND DIVORCE

> When Islam prohibits something, it closes all avenues of approach to it...

The Lawful and the Prohibited in Islam.

> **The woman and the man guilty of adultery and fornication, flog each of them with a hundred stripes: let not compassion move you in their case, in a matter prescribed by God.**

Surah 24:2

> **Nor come nigh to adultery for it is a shameful deed and an evil opening the road to other evils.**

Surah 17:32

Islamic attitudes to sex outside marriage

Sex before marriage is totally forbidden by Islam. The Qur'an forbids sex before marriage and states that men and women should be kept separate socially once puberty has begun. Islam sees no difference between adultery and sex before marriage. The only sex which Islam permits is that between a husband and wife and so all sex outside marriage is the same as adultery.

Islam has strict dress rules for outside the home to make sure that sex outside marriage is not encouraged. Both men and women must wear baggy clothes which do not reveal any sexual features and women should have their hair covered. It is hoped that if men and women are not allowed to mix socially and no one wears clothes to attract the opposite sex, there will be no sex outside marriage.

Any form of cohabitation is therefore banned by Islam.

Islamic attitudes to marriage

All Muslims are expected to marry because the Prophet Muhammad was married and Muslims regard Muhammad as the perfect example of how to live.

The Islamic banning of social contact between Muslims after puberty means that most couples meet through introductions from their parents (arranged marriages). It is felt that these are more likely to work out because the parents choose carefully to make sure the couple are compatible. However, Muslim magazines and newspapers have personal columns where young Muslims advertise for partners. Muslims tend to be married young because this is the best way to prevent sex outside marriage.

All Muslims agree that marriage is a contract which is ideally for life, but there are some differences among Muslims. Most Muslims believe in monogamy, but some accept polygamy. Most Muslims disapprove of divorce, but some do not.

The religious nature of marriage is shown by the fact that Muslim women may only marry Muslim men and Muslim men may only marry Muslim, Jewish or Christian women (as these worship Allah and it is hoped that Jews and Christians will adopt the faith of their husband).

> The selection of marriage partners between Muslims is often regarded as old-fashioned by non-Muslims. Because Islam emphasises chastity and modesty, there is normally very little social contact between young Muslim men and women ... there is no such thing as dating or pre-marital intimacy of any kind. In Islam, sexual behaviour and acts are only for those legally married within the security of marriage.

What does Islam say? Ibrahim Hewitt.

The purpose of marriage in Islam

Muslims believe that marriage is a gift from God which was given:
a) for a woman and man to share love and companionship;
b) for a man and woman to enjoy sex with each other in the way God intended;
c) so that children can be brought into the world;
d) so that children can be brought up in a Muslim family and become good Muslims;
e) it is also a way for Muslims to follow the example of the Prophet Muhammad.

The main features of a Muslim wedding ceremony

Although only the first two features are compulsory, most Muslim weddings in the UK will include all four:
1 There must be a declaration in front of witnesses by each partner that they are entering the marriage freely and without compulsion.
2 The couple must sign a marriage contract which specifies the gift (mahr) given by the groom to the bride which remains the bride's property unless she later chooses to leave her husband.
3 An imam (prayer leader) gives a khutbah and readings from the Qur'an on marriage and leads special prayers for the couple.
4 There is a wedding feast with lots of guests to make the marriage public.

Some Muslims in the UK now have a Muslim wedding service with an exchange of vows. All Muslims must have a registry office wedding as well as a Muslim wedding because British law says that a wedding must have an exchange of vows and be registered. There is a mosque in Cardiff which has been licensed to perform Muslim marriages with an exchange of vows and so a couple married there do not need a registry office wedding.

The bride has her part in the ceremony.

Almighty God created humanity, male and female, each in need of the other, and established the institution of marriage as a means of uniting souls in blessed bond of love, leading to their pleasure and happiness in a way advantageous to mankind. In His Holy Book our Lord says: 'It is He Who has created man from water, and made him kindred of blood and marriage. Your Lord is All Powerful.

From the ceremonial *khutbah* (sermon) preached before the signing of the contracts; published by The Muslim Students' Association of the United States and Canada.

I, Ismail, take Rahila as my lawfully married wife before Allah and in the presence of these witnesses, in accordance with the teachings of the Holy Qur'an. I promise to do everything to make this marriage an act of obedience to Allah, to make it a relationship of love, mercy, peace and faithfulness. Let Allah be my witness, for He is the best of all witnesses.

From a Muslim marriage ceremony recorded in *Milestones,* C Collinson and C. Miller.

> **And among His signs is this, that He created for you mates from among yourselves, that ye may dwell in tranquility with them, and He has put love and mercy between your hearts.**

Surah 20:21

> **Then marry such women as seem good to you, two, three or four at a time. If you fear you will not act justly, then marry one woman only... that is more likely to keep you from committing an injustice.**

Surah 4:3

Muslim men can marry up to four wives at a time. However, some Muslim scholars say that Surah 4:3, and another command in the Qur'an to treat all wives equally, means that polygamy is not possible. Others argue that it is better to have polygamy than to divorce and have single parent families.

Muslim Attitudes to Divorce

Divorce is allowed in Islam but the Qur'an has many regulations about what must happen after divorce. If a man divorces his wife, he must indicate his intention to divorce on three separate occasions with a month in between. During this time attempts should be made by both families to bring about a reconciliation. The couple must live together, but sleep separately, for three months to make sure the wife is not pregnant and to give more chance for reconciliation. At the end of this time both partners are free to marry someone else, but the husband must provide for his wife and children until she re-marries. If a woman divorces her husband, she must repay the mahr and gets nothing from her husband – though he must provide for the children. If either partner ceases to be a Muslim, then the marriage is regarded as ended and divorce is automatic.

The Prophet Muhammad said, 'Among all lawful things, divorce is most hated by Allah.' This, and the fact that marriages are arranged by families who therefore try to make them work, means that many Muslims do not think of divorce, though the divorce rate is growing among British Muslims.

An Egyptian Muslim wedding – all the females are family members.

Jewish attitudes to sex outside marriage

The Torah and the Talmud both teach that sex is only to be enjoyed within marriage. Sex is good, but it is holy because it is a gift from God. Since sex is holy, it must be restricted to the holy state of marriage. The Hebrew word for marriage – kiddushin – means 'made holy'.

This means there can be no sex before marriage for Jews. Orthodox families keep males and females separate after puberty and have arranged marriages. However, some Reform and Progressive Jews accept that there is now a different attitude to sex before marriage and would not condemn a couple living together in a stable relationship as long as they restrict sex to each other and intend to marry and have children.

All Jews condemn sex after marriage with anyone but your marriage partner. Adultery is condemned in the Ten Commandments and elsewhere in the Tenakh and Talmud.

Jewish attitudes to marriage

All Jews are expected to marry and have children because God said several times in the Torah that humans should be fruitful and increase the number of humans on earth. This can only be done by marrying and having a family.

All Jews agree that sex should be kept within marriage and that marriage should be for life. However, they differ as to whether marriages should be arranged, the grounds for divorce and whether men and women should be equal in divorce arrangements.

A Jewish wedding ceremony can only take place between two Jews, and so, if a Jew is to marry a non-Jew in a Jewish wedding, the non-Jew needs to convert.

The purpose of Jewish marriage

Jews believe that marriage is a gift from God which was given:
a) for a man and woman to share love and companionship;
b) for a woman and man to share sex with each other in the way God wants;
c) so that children can be brought into the world and continue the Jewish race;
d) to form a Jewish home so that children can be brought up as Jews and continue the Jewish faith;
e) to obey the commands of God to marry and have children.

JEWISH TEACHING ON MARRIAGE AND DIVORCE

You shall not commit adultery.

Exodus 20:14

Your wife has been given to you in order that you may realise with her life's great plan. A man who has no wife is doomed to an existence without joy, without blessing, without experiencing life's true goodness, without Torah, without protection and without peace.

Talmud

The man said, 'This is now bone of my bones, flesh of my flesh; she shall be called woman for she was taken out of man.' For this reason a man will leave his father and mother and be united to his wife and they will become one flesh.

Genesis 2:23-24

The main features of a Jewish wedding ceremony

There are many variations in Jewish wedding ceremonies between Orthodox and Reform and Shepardim and Ashkenazim, but the main features are:

1 Fasting before the wedding and wearing white as a sign that all the couple's past sins will be forgiven by the marriage;

2 The bride and groom meet under the huppah (canopy) and the bride then circles the groom seven times;

3 Wine is blessed and drunk;

4 The groom puts a ring on the bride's index finger with the words – 'Behold you are consecrated to me with this ring according to the Law of Moses and Israel' (this is what legalises the marriage according to the halakhah);

5 The marriage contract – *ketubah* – is read and given to the bride (the ketubah states the husband's agreement to provide for his wife and specifies her share in the husband's estate in the event of divorce or his death, though many Reform and Liberal Jews just have a marriage certificate as the ketubah);

6 Seven blessings are recited over a second glass of wine;

7 After drinking the wine the groom smashes the glass.

Jewish weddings must have a feast and celebration.

The huppah is a symbol of the couple's new home and unites them under one roof. The fact that it is closed on top and open at the sides symbolises how marriage needs both privacy and openness to friends and community.

The breaking of the glass symbolises the destruction of the Temple in 70 CE reminding the couple of the sadness of Jewish history. It may also symbolise the fact that 'as one step shatters the glass, so one act of unfaithfulness will destroy the holiness and happiness of the home.' Others suggest that the smashing of the glass is permanent and so too the marriage should last for infinity.

The seven blessings include blessing God for wine, creation, making humans, making marriage, making children, and making the bride and groom rejoice. The seventh blessing is:

> Blessed art thou, O Lord our God, King of the universe who hast created joy and gladness, bridegroom and bride, mirth and exultation, pleasure and delight, love, brotherhood, peace and fellowship. Soon O Lord, our God, may there be heard in the streets of Jerusalem, the voice of joy and gladness, the voice of the bridegroom and the voice of the bride, the jubilant voice of bridegrooms from their canopies, and of youths from their feasts of song. Blessed art thou, O Lord, who makest the bridegroom to rejoice with the bride.

The Authorised Daily Prayer Book.

Jewish Teaching on Divorce

Since marriage is an agreement Judaism allows for divorce.

In order to remarry in an Orthodox or Reform synagogue a divorced Jew must have a 'get'. This is a certificate of divorce as specified in Deuteronomy 24 and must be written and given by the Bet Din (group of three senior rabbis). In Orthodox Judaism only a man can give his wife a get, but it is expected that he will not refuse a wife's request for a get. In January 1996 all Orthodox Jews in Britain were ordered to have nothing to do with a man because he refused to give his wife a get.

Reform Bet Din allow a wife to ask for a divorce. Liberal Jews do not have religious divorce, but just accept civil divorce. The reasons which permit a divorce in Judaism are very similar to the civil divorce laws of the UK. However, a couple must wait three months before a divorce is complete in case the wife is pregnant.

Nevertheless, Judaism discourages divorce and encourages couples to stay together for life.

> If a man marries a woman who becomes displeasing to him because he finds something indecent about her... he writes her a certificate of divorce.

Deuteronomy 24:1

> If a man divorces his first wife – even the altar (of the Temple) sheds tears.

Talmud

> Thus do I set you free, release you, and put you aside, in order that you may have permission and authority over yourself to go and marry any man you may desire. No person may hinder you from this day onward and you are permitted to every man.

Extract from an *Orthodox get*.

HINDU TEACHING ON MARRIAGE AND DIVORCE

Hindu attitudes to sex outside marriage

Hindus see sex as a wonderful gift from God. However, they believe that sex should be restricted to marriage. Sex is a part of the householder stage of life, and being a householder means being married. Sex is not allowed before you become a householder because the first stage of life is that of a student of Hinduism in which sex is not allowed. Sex has to be given up when Hindus enter the third stage of life.

Adultery is not allowed in Hinduism because it means not only betraying your partner, but also betraying your dharma and so preventing you from attaining moksha. As marriage is also seen as the union of two families, adultery would be very serious as it would break the family union.

> **O, married men and women; be loving and faithful to one another.**

Shikshapatri of Lord Swaminarayan.

> Hinduism emphasises the positive value of human sexuality, and by depicting ideal relationships (e.g. between Krishna and Radha, or between Rama and Sita in the Ramayana) it offers an image of religious devotion and examples for people to follow.

Guidelines for Life, Mel Thompson.

Hindu attitudes to marriage

For Hindus, marriage is a religious stage of life passing from the student to the householder. All Hindus see marriage as religious and most regard it as for life, although some Hindus accept divorce.

Traditionally a Hindu marriage should be carried out by a priest between two members of the same caste. For this reason Hindu marriages tend to be arranged. However, as there are no great restrictions on the mixing of men and women, many British Hindus find their own marriage partners.

A Hindu wedding.

The purpose of marriage in Hinduism

Hindus believe that marriage is a gift from God which was given:
a) to allow you to fulfil your role as a householder;
b) for a woman and man to share love and companionship;
c) to have the joy of sex in the way of Hinduism (dharma);
d) to have the joy of children;
e) to bring the union of two families.

The main features of a Hindu wedding ceremony

There are great varieties between Hindu wedding ceremonies, but the main features are likely to be:

1 Prayers and hymns about the joys of marriage;

2 Offerings to the gods;

3 The bride standing on a stone to represent the stability marriage brings;

4 The throwing rice into the sacred fire (havan) to encourage fertility in the bride and groom;

5 The couple taking seven steps around the sacred fire – this is the essential part of marriage laid down by the Law Code of Manu;

6 The groom placing a black and gold necklace round the bride's neck to represent the union of their two families.

Hindu teaching on divorce

Divorce and remarriage are rare in Hinduism – the main grounds for divorce are cruelty or not having children after 15 years. The connection of marriage to the family and the extended family adds to the forces keeping couples together. Nevertheless divorce is occurring more frequently both in India and in the Hindu community in the UK, perhaps as they become more affluent and westernised, and as women receive more rights and are less likely to accept bad behaviour (e.g. adultery) from their husbands.

> Take the first step for the sake of food,
> Take the second for strength,
> Take the third for wealth,
> Take the fourth for happiness,
> Take the fifth for children,
> Take the sixth for sustenance'
> Take the seventh for unity

The seven steps.

> She is given as a collaborator in the performance of duties which a householder ought to perform. She is to inspire and stimulate and she is to lead you on in the path of dharma

Words of the bride's father in the marriage service.

> You and I accept each other with understanding and complete love. You are like soil and I am like the sun; come, let us marry and have children.

Husband's promise.

Wedding dolls symbolise that Hindu marriages are meant to last.

CHRISTIANITY AND THE FAMILY

The family is the original cell of social life. It is the natural society in which husband and wife are called to give themselves in love and in the gift of life. . . . The family is the community in which, from childhood, one can learn moral values, begin to honour God and make good use of freedom. Family life is an initiation into life in society.

Catechism of the Catholic Church.

How being a Christian may help in the upbringing of children

1 The Christian marriage service and the Christian purpose of marriage encourage parents to bring up their children as good Christians.

2 Christian marriage is for life and so Christian parents will stay together giving their children a stable home life.

3 Christian parents will have their children baptised (or dedicated if they believe in adult baptism). At this service the parents promise to provide a Christian home of love and faithfulness for their children.

4 Christianity teaches that the family is extremely important and that parents and children have duties to each other. Parents have a duty to care for their children and bring them up as Christians. Children have a duty to respect their parents when they are young and to care for their parents when they are older.

5 By taking their children to Church and/or Sunday School, parents will make sure that their children are given Christian teachings about right and wrong and this should improve their behaviour and lead to them becoming good citizens.

Children obey your parents in the Lord, for this is right. 'Honour your father and mother' – which is the first commandment with a promise – 'that it may go well with you and that you may enjoy long life on the earth.' Fathers do not exasperate your children; instead, bring them up in the training and instruction of the Lord.

Ephesians 6:1–4

A baby being anointed with chrism at a Roman Catholic baptism.

How churches help family life

Christians believe all children have a right to family life and so they encourage married couples who cannot have children to adopt unwanted children and they encourage Christian families to foster children in care. The National Children's Home (Methodist Church) and the Children's Society (Church of England) were founded to provide something near to family life for children who did not have it.

Almost all Christian churches hold Family Services which unite the family and give them an opportunity to discover religion together. Services at festivals such as Christmas and Easter also give an opportunity for family togetherness. Churches also run Sunday Schools giving children teachings on behaviour and beliefs.

There are Church Schools (mainly Roman Catholic and Church of England) which try to give the family more help in giving their children a Christian upbringing.

Churches run many activities to give children and young people a moral social life. Brownies, Guides, Beavers, Cubs, Scouts, Girls' Brigade and Boys' Brigade are usually based in churches. Most churches also run youth clubs and youth fellowships.

Ian Ramsey Church of England Comprehensive School.

Christians provide many charities to help with family life, for example – Catholic Marriage Advisory Council, National Catholic Child Welfare Council.

Christians are expected to care for their parents when they are no longer capable of caring for themselves.

Many Churches run homes for old people e.g. Methodist Homes for the Aged.

> **Honour your father and your mother so that you may live long in the land the Lord your God is giving you.**
>
> *Exodus 20:12*

> However, the family is not an end in itself. While parents are to be honoured, they are not always to be obeyed. All must leave one home to found another, either with others or as a single person. Human fulfilment is possible without marriage and without engaging in sexual intercourse. Singleness offers opportunities for friendship and service which are not open to married people.

Statement from the Methodist Church in *What the Churches Say on Moral Issues*.

> The fourth commandment reminds grown children of their responsibilities towards their parents. As much as they can, they must give them material and moral support in old age and in times of illness, loneliness or distress.

Catechism of the Catholic Church.

ISLAM AND THE FAMILY

No father can give his child anything better than good manners.

Hadith quoted by al'Timmidhi.

Be careful of your duty to Allah and be fair and just to your children.

Hadith quoted by al'Bukhari.

Your riches and your children may be but a trial.

Surah 64:15

How being a Muslim may help in the upbringing of children

1 The Muslim purpose of marriage encourages parents to bring up their children as good Muslims.

2 Islam sees the family as a vital part of society and Muslim parents are expected to give their children a stable family life.

3 Islam teaches that children are a gift from God and that Muslims will be judged on how they treat their children. This should help them to be serious about their roles as parents.

4 At the Aqiqa (a naming ceremony when a Muslim child is a few days old), Muslim parents promise to bring up their children as good Muslims.

5 Bringing a child up as a Muslim, going to mosque and madrasah will give the child Muslim teachings about right and wrong which should improve their behaviour and lead them to become good citizens.

6 Islam teaches that parents and children have duties to each other. Parents must look after their children materially and bring them up as good Muslims. Children must respect their parents and look after them when they are old.

7 Muslim inheritance laws, based on the Qur'an, keep the extended family together by ensuring that at least two thirds of an estate is left to the family.

A Muslim family celebrate an engagement (betrothal).

How the Mosque helps family life

Salah does not have to be done in the mosque, and most Muslim women say all their prayers at home. Children learn to pray at home and for many Muslims prayers are said as a family. The Muslim festivals are centred on the home and it is from the home that young Muslims learn about halal and haram.

All mosques run mosque schools (madrasahs) for boys and girls. They are held on weeknights and Sundays and teach children about Islam, how to read the Qur'an in Arabic and how Muslims should behave. There are now many Muslim schools to provide separate education for boys and girls and to teach children the National Curriculum in a Muslim way. Most of these schools have to be paid for, but a few are now funded by the state in the same way as Church Schools.

Help in the case of marriage breakdown comes from the two families, the imam and Muslim lawyers. The zakah fund helps families with financial difficulties and many mosques have a family committee to help Muslim families in trouble.

The Al'Madinah Mosque in Batley, Yorkshire.

Paradise lies at the feet of your mother.

Hadith quoted by Sunan an'Nasa'i.

We have enjoined on man kindness to his parents: in pain did his mother bear him, and in pain did she give him birth. The carrying of the child to its weaning is thirty months. At length when he reaches the age of full strength and attains forty years, he says, 'O my Lord! Grant me that I may be grateful for thy favour which Thou hast bestowed upon me and upon both my parents, and that I may work righteousness.'

Surah 46:15

A man asked Prophet Muhammad, peace be upon him, 'O Messenger of Allah! Who deserves the best care from me?' The Prophet said, 'Your mother.' He asked, 'Who then?' The Prophet said, 'Your mother.' The man asked yet again, 'Who then?' Prophet Muhammad said, 'Your mother.' The man asked once more, 'Who then?' The Prophet said, 'Your father.'

Hadith quoted by al'Bukhari.

JUDAISM AND THE FAMILY

How being a Jew may help in the upbringing of children

1 The Jewish marriage service and the Jewish purpose of marriage encourage parents to bring up their children as good Jews.

2 The Shabbat ceremonies and the festivals are centred on the home so bringing the family closer together.

3 Keeping kashrut means that meals, cooking etc. always remind the children of Judaism.

4 Jewish parents are encouraged to teach their children how to be good Jews in the circumcision and/or thanksgiving service after babies are born.

5 The Torah commands children to respect their parents and look after them when they are old.

6 Bringing children up as Jews and going to synagogue school (heder) will give them Jewish teachings about right and wrong. This should improve their behaviour and lead to them becoming good citizens.

> **Honour your father and your mother that you may live long in the land the Lord your God is giving you.**
>
> *Exodus 20:12*

> **Honour your father and mother, as the Lord your God has commanded you,**
>
> *Deutronomy 5:16*

> May the All-merciful bless the father and mother of the child; may they be worthy to rear him, to initiate him in the precepts of the Law, and to train him in wisdom: from this eighth day and henceforth may his blood be accepted and may the Lord his God be with him.

Service at a circumcision from *The Authorised Daily Prayer Book.*

Jewish families always meet together for the Shabbat meal.

How the Synagogue helps with family life

All synagogues provide lessons in Hebrew and Judaism for the children (heder) which help with the Jewish upbringing of the children. The services in synagogues on Sabbath and festivals bring the family closer by worshipping together (though males and females sit separately in Orthodox synagogues).

Synagogues also provide social activities for children and young people so that they can have a moral social life. These include youth clubs (separate for boys and girls in Orthodox synagogues) and uniformed organisations.

There are also Jewish schools where the National Curriculum is taught in a Jewish way. Many of these are funded by the state like Christian schools.

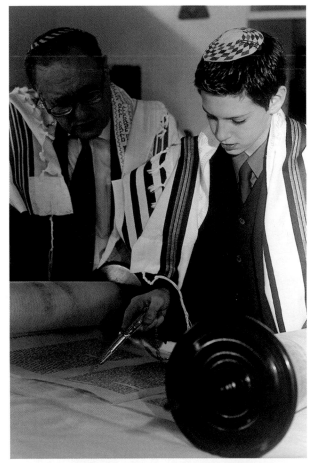

A Jewish boy has his Bar Mitzvah after being taught his religious duties.

The Jewish marriage service and all the religious activities centred on the home are aimed at helping families to stay together. In addition, most Jewish communities run a family agency committee to help with family problems and to provide interest-free loans to families in need; rabbis provide counselling for marriage problems and there are many Jewish retirement homes subsidised by Jewish charities e.g. Jewish Care.

Hear, O Israel: the Lord our God, the Lord is one. Love the Lord your God with all your heart and with all your soul and with all your strength. These commandments that I give you today are to be upon your hearts. Impress them on your children. Talk about them when you sit at home and when you walk along the road, when you lie down and when you get up. Tie them as symbols on your hands and bind them on your foreheads. Write them on the doorframes of your houses and on your gates.

Deuteronomy 6:4-9 (The Shema)

Bestow thy blessing upon thy handmaid; strengthen and uphold me together with my husband that we may rear the child that has been born unto us to fear thee and to serve thee in truth, and to walk in the path of righteousness. Keep the tender babe in all his(her) ways. Favour him (her) with knowledge, understanding and discernment, and let his(her) portion be in thy law, so that he(she) may sanctify thy great name and become a comfort to us in our old age.

Prayer from the service of thanksgiving after childbirth, *The Authorised Daily Prayer*

HINDUISM AND THE FAMILY

The great Epics depicted what was in many ways the ideal: children were shown as dutiful to parents, parents as attached to their children, wives and husbands in relations of mutual respect; love and harmony as present everywhere. Hence the Epics served – and to a great extent still serve – as paradigms (examples) of ideal behaviour for the common man with his family.

Hinduism, Hinnells and Sharpe.

May we be happy with offspring. May we be blessed with dharma. Bless us, protect us and help us to respect elders and follow a righteous path for ever. Give us strength to follow the path of the householder, the man to become a gentleman and the woman to be an ideal wife. May our children behave in the same way.

Hymn at Marriage.

How being a Hindu can help in the upbringing of children

1 Family life is a central part of Hindu life. By bringing children up well, you fulfil your dharma. As this is essential for salvation (moksha), it encourages parents to bring up their children well.

2 Hindu stories in the Ramayana, Mahabharata and Puranas show parents how Hindu life should be lived.

3 Worship is centred on the home and Hindus should worship every day in the household shrine. This brings the family together as a unit.

4 Special worship on the anniversary of the death of a family member helps children to realise the nature of the extended family.

5 Hinduism teaches that children should respect their parents and look after them when they are old.

6 Bringing children up in Hinduism teaches them about right and wrong, and should improve their behaviour and help them to become good citizens.

Family life is very important in Hinduism and Hindu families always worship together.

How the Mandir helps with the upbringing of children

Most Hindu temples (mandir) run classes on Sundays or in the evenings to teach young Hindus about their faith. It is also expected that Hindu parents will bring their children with them to the mandir for worship and for festivals.

The mandir also has a haveli which provides all sorts of social activities including children's and young people's groups, where young Hindus can have a moral social life.

There are now some Hindu day schools where Hindus can follow the National Curriculum in a Hindu way. As yet these schools have not been given any state funding.

School assembly at the Swaminarayan Independent Day School, Neasden.

> **Where the women are respected, there lives God. If the wife is obedient to the husband and the husband loves his wife; if the children obey the parents, and guests are entertained; if the family duty is performed and gifts are given to the needy, then there is heaven and nowhere else.**

Law of Manu

> There is an expression in Hinduism that your father is an image of the Lord of Creation and your mother is an image of the Earth. Honouring them is therefore a person's first duty; and if you fail to do so, then all other religious duties are useless.

Guidelines for Life, Mel Thompson.

> Serve your parents in their old age and take good care of them, especially in their illness.

Shikshapatri of Lord Swaminarayan.

The importance of family life in religion

The way that parents are helped in the upbringing of their children by being a member of a religion and by the church or mosque, or synagogue, or mandir shows that religion considers family life to be important.

The family is at the heart of all the religions covered in this book because they believe the family was created by God as the way of passing their religion onto a new generation.

QUESTIONS

Factfile 1 Social facts on marriage, divorce and the family

1 What is cohabitation and is it becoming more popular?

2 What is the difference between cohabiting and marriage?

3 Why might some people say serial monogamy is not much different from promiscuity?

4 What evidence is there that marriage is becoming less popular?

5 Why was there a big increase in divorce between 1961 and 1981?

6 What evidence is there that there has been an increase in one-parent families?

7 Give three reasons why divorce may not be a good idea.

Factfile 2 Christian teaching on marriage and divorce

1 Have a classroom discussion on whether marriage is better than cohabitation from a Christian point of view.

2 Write down the Christian reasons against divorce and the Christian reasons in favour of divorce. Come to a conclusion on whether you are in favour of divorce, and, if so, in what circumstances.

Factfiles 3, 4, 5 Muslim, Jewish and Hindu teaching on marriage and divorce

1 Choose one of these religions and write down:
(a) whether or not it opposes cohabitation, and, if so, why;
(b) the purposes of marriage according to that religion;
(c) what that religion teaches about divorce and why.

2 'Having a religious wedding ceremony makes no difference to how the marriage works out.' Do you agree? Give reasons for your opinion, showing you have considered another point of view.

3 Have a class discussion on whether religious marriages are more likely to last than registry office marriages.

Factfile 6 Christianity and the family

1 Give three reasons why Christians consider the family important.

2 Describe three ways in which Christianity helps a family to stay together.

Factfiles 7, 8, 9 Islam, Judaism, Hinduism and the family

1 Choose one religion and give three reasons why family life is important to that religion.

2 Describe three ways in which the religion helps parents with the upbringing of their children.

3 'Without religion, family life will collapse.' Do you agree? Give reasons for your opinion, showing you have considered another point of view.

SOCIAL HARMONY

Women in the UK have always had the right to own property and earn their own living, but they did not have the same rights as men and when women married, their husbands had the right to use their property. During the second half of the nineteenth century it became the accepted view that married women should stay at home and look after the children (in 1850 about 50 per cent of married women had been in employment, but by 1900 this was down to about 15 per cent). The two world wars (where women had to do men's jobs and did them very well) and the various women's movements wanting equal rights for women have changed the attitude to the roles of men and women in the UK and it is now generally accepted that men and women are equal.

FACTFILE 10

SOCIAL FACTS CONCERNING THE ROLES OF MEN AND WOMEN

TABLE 1 WOMEN'S RIGHTS

1882 – The Married Women's Property Act allowed married women to keep their property separate from their husband's.

1892 – The Local Government Act allowed women the vote in local elections and the right to stand as councillors.

1918 – The Representation of the People Act allowed women over 31 to vote in parliamentary elections (men could vote at 21).

1928– Electoral Reform Act gave the vote to women over 21 and allowed women to stand as MP's.

1970 – The Equal Pay Act required employers to give women the same pay as men – Equal pay for like work regardless of the employee's sex.

1975 – Sex Discrimination Act made it illegal to discriminate in jobs on grounds of sex or whether a person is married.

TABLE 2 EMPLOYMENT BY GENDER

| | Males (thousands) | | Females (thousands) | |
	Full-time	Part-time	Full-time	Part-time
1984	13 240	570	5422	4343
1989	14 071	734	6336	4907
1994	12 875	998	6131	5257
1997	13 380	1328	6592	5367

Source: Social Trends 28.

In 1970 women's earnings were 63.1 per cent of men's. By 1985 they were 74.1 per cent of men's.

CHRISTIANITY AND THE ROLES OF MEN AND WOMEN

> Wives submit to your husbands as to the Lord. For the husband is the head of the wife as Christ is the head of the church. Now as the church submits to Christ, so also wives should submit to their husbands in everything... However, each one of you also must love his wife as he loves himself, and the wife must respect her husband.

Ephesians 5:22-24,33

> A woman should learn in quietness and full submission. I do not permit a woman to teach or to have authority over a man; she must be silent. For Adam was formed first, then Eve. And Adam was not the one deceived; it was the woman who was deceived.

1 Timothy 2:11-14

> So God created man in his own image, in the image of God he created him, male and female he created them.

Genesis 1:27

Christianity has different attitudes to the roles of men and women.

The traditional roles in Christianity

Many Evangelical Protestants teach that men and women have separate and different roles. It is the role of women to bring up children and run a Christian home. Women should not speak in church and must submit to their husbands. It is the role of men to provide for the family and to lead the family in religion. Men must love their wives as themselves, but only men can be church leaders and teachers.

This teaching is based on the teachings of St Paul about women not being allowed to teach or speak in church, the teaching of Genesis 2 about Adam being created first, and other biblical teachings.

The modern roles in Christianity

Many Protestant Churches now accept that men and women are equal, and they have women ministers and priests (e.g. Church of England, Methodist, URC, Baptist). These Churches teach that men and women have equal roles.

This teaching is based on the teachings of Genesis 1 that male and female were created at the same time and equally; the teaching of St Paul that in Christ there is neither male nor female. It is especially based on the evidence from the gospels that Jesus treated women as his equals. He preached in the court of women in the Jerusalem Temple (Matthew 21:23–22:14). He treated a Samaritan woman as his equal (John 4). He had women disciples who stayed with him at the cross (Matthew 27:55, Mark 15:40–41, Luke 23:27, John 25:27) unlike the male disciples who ran away. It was to women that Jesus appeared first after the resurrection. There is even evidence that there were women priests in the early Church as they must have existed to be banned by the Council of Laodicea in the fourth century.

The roles of men and women in Roman Catholic Christianity

The Roman Catholic Church teaches that men and women are completely equal and should have equal roles in life. This is based on the same biblical teachings as the modern roles and on the teachings of the Catholic Catechism.

However, the Catholic Church does not allow women priests because it regards all priests as the successors of the apostles of Jesus, and as Jesus only appointed men as apostles, only men can be priests.

> The Lord Jesus chose men to form the college of the twelve apostles, and the apostles did the same when they chose collaborators to succeed them in their ministry... For this reason the ordination of women is not possible.

Catechism of the Catholic Church.

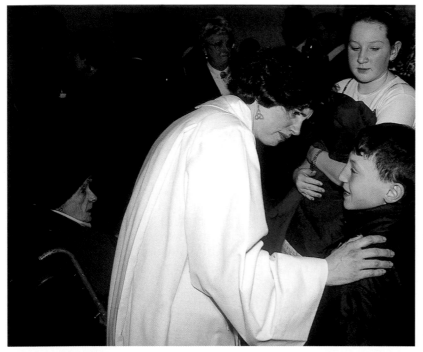

Most Protestant Churches now say that the role of men and women in religion is totally equal. The Methodist, Baptist, United Reformed and the Church of England all have women ministers/priests.

There is neither Jew nor Greek, slave nor free, male nor female, for you are all one in Christ Jesus.

Galatians 3:28

> Wilt thou have this man to thy wedded husband, to live together after God's ordinance in the holy estate of matrimony? Wilt thou obey him and serve him, honour and keep him in sickness and in health; and forsaking all other, keep thee only unto him, so long as ye both shall live?

Church of England Marriage Service 1662.

> N will you take N to be your husband? Will you love him, comfort him, honour and protect him, and, forsaking all others, be faithful to him so long as you both shall live.

Church of England Alternative Service Book, 1980.

> A wife is to submit graciously to the servant leadership of her husband even as the Church willingly submits to the leadership of Christ ... she, being in the image of God, as is her husband and thus equal to him, has the God-given responsibility to respect her husband and to serve as his helper.

The Southern Baptist Convention of the USA, June 1998.

ISLAM AND THE ROLES OF MEN AND WOMEN

Whoever works righteousness, man or woman... verily to him will We give a new life.

Surah 16:97

The search for knowledge is a duty for every Muslim, male or female.

Hadith quoted by al'Bukhari.

Women have the same rights in relation to their husbands as are expected in all decency of them; while men stand a step above them.

Surah 2:228

Men are the ones who support women since God has given some persons advantages over others.

Surah 4:34

Islam teaches that men and women are completely equal in religion and that both men and women have an equal right to education.

However, Islam does not believe that equal means the same. Men and women have different roles in Islam because God has given them a different biological nature and different biological functions. God created women to have children and bring them up, and so the principal role for women in Islam is to keep a halal (good Muslim) home and bring up the children. God gave men a stronger physique and so the role of men in Islam is to go out to work in a halal way to provide the financial support for the home. Both men and women have the role of bringing up the children to be good Muslims.

These different roles mean that males and females have a slightly different status, for example a woman only inherits half of what a man does. This is because the man has to provide the financial support for the family.

Islam recognises the biological differences between men and women so although they are equal, they are not the same... In western society, where the obvious biological differences between men and women are overlooked in the quest for equality, the destabilising effect this is having is plain for all to see: broken marriages, illegitimate children and the breakdown of family life can all be said to rise, at least in part, from the move away from and non-acceptance of the traditional roles for men and women... Education is a right for women as well as men and all should have the opportunity to study at the highest levels, the only condition being that their modesty is not put at risk within the study situation. In other words the Islamic guidance on dress and the limits on free mixing with strangers must be observed and preserved. The same applies to the issue of whether women can seek employment or not. Clearly there are occupations which would make it impossible for the Islamic codes to be followed and so women should not seek employment in those jobs (for example as fashion models).

What does Islam say? Ibrahim Hewitt.

This Muslim police officer in Oman wears a long skirt in order to be correctly dressed.

The Jewish laws (*mitzvot*) are taken by Orthodox Jews to apply mainly to men. The rabbis exempted women from all the mitzvot applied to a particular time (except eating no leaven at Pesach and fasting on Yom Kippur) because they recognised the obligation of women to look after their families. Until fairly recently Jewish women married early, had many children and spent most of their lives raising small children so they did not have time to attend synagogue and fulfil the ritual functions.

So in Orthodox Judaism today women cannot form a *minyan* (the number of Jews needed for a synagogue service) and cannot say the ritual prayers either at home or in the synagogue unless a man is present. Women must sit separately from men in the synagogue and they are not allowed to study the Talmud at the highest levels. Orthodox women cannot initiate divorce, cannot remarry if their husband refuses to divorce them and cannot be a witness in a Jewish court.

This is because the role of women in Judaism is to keep a kosher home and bring up the family; and the role of men is to provide for the family and fulfil all the mitzvot given to Jewish men by God.

The Orthodox believe this way of life is the best for social harmony because it allows family life to develop in the way God wanted.

In Reform and Progressive Judaism, there is a totally different attitude. Women have complete equality. They pray with men, they can form a minyan, they can be rabbis (e.g. Julia Neuberger), they can initiate divorce and they can be witnesses in court. This is only possible because the Reform and Progressive Jews refuse to follow the Torah and Talmud literally.

FACTFILE 13

JUDAISM AND THE ROLES OF MEN AND WOMEN

> To the woman he said, 'I will greatly increase your pains in childbearing; with pain you will give birth to children. Your desire will be for your husband and he will rule over you.'

Genesis 3:16

Times have changed. Women do not marry young, do not have many children. They lead their own lives as single, married or divorced women and it is up to Reform Judaism to re-interpret the Torah in the light of these changes.

The First Jewish Catalogue.

Rabbi Sylvia Rothschild prepares a girl for her Bat Mitzvah.

FACTFILE 14

HINDUISM AND THE ROLES OF MEN AND WOMEN

The father protects the woman in childhood, the husband protects her in youth, the children protect her in old age, a woman should never be independent.

Law of Manu

Go to your husband's home and take charge of it. Occupy the main position and carry out all the activities connected with the home. Here may you have children and protect your happiness.

Hindu Marriage Service.

Traditional Hinduism sees the role of men as the protector of women and women as child bearers and rearers and homemakers.

However, these attitudes have changed with many Hindus and several Hindu sects have different ideas on the role of men and women. Iskcon (Hare Krishna), the Virashaivas (Lingayats) and the Swaminarayan Hindu Mission treat men and women equally and think they have an equal role to play in religion and life.

Soon after Indian independence, women were given equality before the law and equal voting rights and for many years India had a woman prime minister, Indira Gandhi.

Rabindranath Tagore (1861–1941) a Hindu writer and winner of the Nobel Prize for Literature in 1913 founded Shantiniketan College for men and women with the words, 'In the future civilisation women will have their place'.

The Women's Wing of the Swaminarayan Hindu Mission, Neasden, at a prayer meeting.

Krishna and other Hindu gods and goddesses are seen as examples of how men and women should treat one another.

The UK has always been a mixed society – Celts, Romans, Angles, Saxons, Jutes, Danes, Vikings, Normans are all ancestors of the English.

The UK has always believed in human freedom and offered asylum to those suffering persecution – to French Protestants (Huguenots) in the seventeenth century, to Russian Jews in the nineteenth century, to European Jews escaping Hitler in the 1930's.

In the nineteenth century the UK built up an overseas empire around the world. In exchange for being ruled by Britain, citizens of the Empire were allowed to settle in the UK.

The Empire became known as the Commonwealth as nations gained their independence from the UK. In the 1950s there was substantial immigration from the Commonwealth. Workers were recruited from India, Pakistan, Bangladesh, West Africa and the Caribbean to lessen a labour shortage in the UK. Many of these workers had fought for the UK in the Second World War (there were more people from the Commonwealth than from the UK in the British Armed Forces in the Second World War).

SOCIAL FACTS CONCERNING THE UK AS A MULTI-ETHNIC SOCIETY

TABLE 1 ETHNIC MINORITIES IN THE UK 1991

Afro–Caribbean	495 000
Indian	787 000
Pakistani	428 000
Bangladeshi	108 000
Chinese	125 000
African	112 000
Mixed	287 000
European/Australian	472 000

Source: Race through the 90s, CRE.

In 1991 only 4.8 per cent of the UK's population was ethnic minority and 50 per cent of these were born in the UK.

The Notting Hill Carnival celebrates the fact that Britain is a multi-ethnic society.

The Race Relations Act 1976

- makes it unlawful to discriminate against anyone because of race, colour, nationality, ethnic or national origins in the sphere of jobs, training, housing, education and the provision of services;

- makes it unlawful to use threatening or abusive or insulting words in public which could stir up racial hatred;

- makes it illegal to publish anything likely to cause racial hatred.

Meena, a young Asian woman with eight GCSE's and three A levels, went for an interview at an insurance firm where her friend, Sally, worked:

> I didn't get the job. But Sally told me they said that, in the recession, it was important to give jobs to your own. Now tell me, what does that mean? I was born here, I speak with a brummie accent.
> My grandfather, like so many others, died fighting for this country - he was in Italy - we even have a letter from his commander about how brave he was.
> My mother works in the health service, my father in insurance. They've never collected a penny in benefits, and have paid taxes for twenty five years. Dad won't even let me go on the dole. So what does 'your own' mean ?

Source: Race through the 90s, CRE.

RACIAL PREJUDICE – THINKING CERTAIN RACES ARE INFERIOR OR SUPERIOR, USUALLY WITHOUT EVIDENCE.

RACIAL DISCRIMINATION – PUTTING PREJUDICE INTO PRACTICE AND TREATING PEOPLE LESS FAVOURABLY BECAUSE OF THEIR RACIAL, NATIONAL, ETHNIC OR COLOUR ORIGINS.

RACISM – THE BELIEF THAT SOME RACES ARE SUPERIOR TO OTHERS, BASED ON SUPPOSED BIOLOGICAL FACTS WHICH SCIENCE HAS SHOWN TO BE UNTRUE.

Equally British – the Bradford Festival in 1996.

TABLE 2 UNEMPLOYMENT RATES BY ETHNIC GROUP SPRING 1994	
White	8%
Indian	15%
Chinese/other ethnic groups/ mixed race	19%
Black (West Indian and African)	26%
Pakistani/Bangladeshi	28%

Source: Social Trends 28.

TABLE 3 RACIAL ATTACKS REPORTED TO THE POLICE		
	1988	1990
England and Wales	4383	6459
Scotland	299	636

Source: Social Trends in the 90s, CRE.

'I believe deeply that all men and women should be able to go as far as talent, ambition and effort can take them. There should be no barriers of background, no barriers of religion, no barriers of race. I want... a society that encourages each and every one to fulfil his or her potential to the utmost... let me say here and now that I regard any barrier built on race to be pernicious...'

Speech by John Major September 1991.

An equal opportunity can make all the difference.

The Commission for Racial Equality was set up by the Government in 1976 to enforce the Race Relations Act. It has three duties:

- to fight against racial discrimination;

- to make people understand the importance of giving everyone an equal chance, whatever their race, colour, ethnic origin or nationality;

- to keep a check on how the law is working, and tell the Government how it could be improved.

CHRISTIANITY AND RACIAL HARMONY

> 'I now realise how true it is that God does not show favouritism, but accepts men from every nation who fear him and do what is right.'

Acts 10:34

Paul said,

> 'From one man he made every nation of men, that they should inhabit the whole earth.'

Acts 17:26

> Here there is no Greek or Jew, circumcised or uncircumcised, barbarian, Scythian, slave or free, but Christ is all in all.

Colossians 3:11

> 'There is neither Jew nor Greek, slave nor free, male nor female, for you are all one in Christ Jesus.'

Galatians 3:28

Christian teachings quite clearly promote racial harmony.

In the Parable of the Good Samaritan (Luke 10:25–37), Jesus taught that Christians should love their neighbours and that neighbour means people of all races. Jews and Samaritans were different races who hated each other. In the parable Jesus taught that the Good Samaritan treated the Jew who was attacked as his neighbour. Also, Jesus treated a Samaritan woman as his equal (John 4); healed a Roman centurion's servant (Luke 7) and had a black African helping him to carry his cross (Luke 23:26).

St Peter was given a vision by God (Acts 10) which showed him that God treats all races the same and accepts the worship of anyone who does right whatever their race.

St Paul taught that everyone is equal in Christ who overcame all the divisions of race. He also taught that as God created all nations from one man, Adam, all nations are therefore equal to each other.

These teachings have been developed by the Churches which have all issued statements condemning racism and encouraging all Christians to live in harmony. In May 1998 the Presidents of Churches Together in England published a letter condemning racism and religious hatred and asking voters and political parties involved in local elections not to be involved in any form of racism.

> Respect for the humanity we share with each and every neighbour is the only basis for a peaceful and good society. Any attack on the dignity and human rights of any racial or religious group damages all of us.

From the Churches Together letter to the press, May 1998.

> There is cause for celebration in church and society when black and white people learn to cooperate, share power and make decisions together and where new forms of community life are thus discovered. The United Reformed Church commits itself to challenge and equip all its people to resist racism within themselves, within the church and within society as a whole and to train people and devote resources to this task.

Declaration on Racism from URC 1987.

The Celestial Church of Christ in Peckham, south London, is Nigerian in origin but provides joyful worship for many races.

> We affirm that racism is a direct contradiction of the gospel of Jesus. We welcome the multi-racial nature of society in Britain and assert our unqualified commitment to it. We regard it as economically, socially and spiritually beneficial for total human development.

Methodist Conference Statement 1987.

ISLAM AND RACIAL HARMONY

> **And among His Signs is the creation of the heavens and the earth, and the variations in your languages and your colours; verily, in that there are Signs for those who know.**

Surah 30:22

> **O mankind, We created you from a single pair of a male and a female, and made you into tribes and nations that you may know each other (not that you despise each other). Verily the most honoured of you in the sight of Allah is he who is the most righteous of you.**

Surah 49:13

> **All mankind is from Adam and Eve, an Arab has no superiority over a non-Arab nor a non-Arab has any superiority over an Arab; also a white has no superiority over black nor a black has any superiority over white except by piety and good action. Learn that every Muslim is a brother to every Muslim and that the Muslims constitute one brotherhood.**

The Prophet Muhammad in his Last Sermon 9 Dhul Hijjah 632.

Islam teaches that all Muslims form one community known as the Ummah. In the last recorded words of the Prophet Muhammad, the Prophet said that every Muslim is a brother to every other Muslim and therefore there can be no form of racism among Muslims.

This can be further seen by the way in which Muhammad chose a black African as his first prayer caller. The multi-racial nature of Islam is clearly seen in the events of Hajj when over two million Muslims of all colours and races join together as one group.

The Qur'an teaches that all humanity was created by God from one pair of humans, therefore all races are equal and none can be despised.

> Racism, whether open or hidden, is an evil aspect of life which Islam seeks to eradicate... The equality of human beings in all matters except piety (which we are encouraged to try to increase) is clear. Under no circumstances can a person be ill-treated or abused simply because they happen to be of a different race. As you can gather, therefore, Muslims are not a distinct racial or ethnic group, to be classified by people as 'Asians' or 'Arabs' to the exclusion of the other races which all belong to the family of Islam.

What does Islam say? Ibrahim Hewitt.

An African kissing the Black Stone.

Judaism teaches that as all humans can be traced back to Adam and Eve, they must all be brothers and sisters. There is only one God and so there is only one humanity.

A rabbi, Ben Azzai, translated Genesis 5:1 as, 'This is the book of the generations of Man' showing that in the Tenakh there is no division of humans into black or white or any races.

The experience by Jews of racial discrimination which led to Hitler's attempt to destroy the Jews in the Holocaust makes it impossible for Jews to regard racism as anything other than evil and very, very dangerous. Although the Jews see themselves as the chosen people of God, this does not mean that they look down on other races or treat them differently. All humans are the creation of God and must be treated as equals, but Jews have been given a special responsibility from God, the responsibility of witnessing God's laws to the rest of humanity.

There is a lot of teaching in the Tenakh about how God cares for the oppressed and how God wants his people to bring justice to the world. This is especially seen in the Book of Amos which many Jews believe teaches them to oppose any form of bad treatment because of race, social class or poverty.

Black Jews are welcomed as immigrants to Israel.

JUDAISM AND RACIAL HARMONY

> **Adam named his wife Eve because she would become the mother of all the living.**

Genesis 3:20

> **Do not abhor an Edomite for he is your brother. Do not abhor an Egyptian because you lived as an alien in his country.**

Deuteronomy 23:7

> **I will keep you and will make you to be a covenant for the people and a light for the Gentiles.**

Isaiah 42:6

> **When an alien lives with you in your land, do not ill-treat him. The alien living with you must be treated as one of your native born.**

Leviticus 19:33-34

Then the Lord God formed man of the dust of the ground.' (Genesis 2:7). 'From which part of the earth's surface did He gather the dust?' ask the Rabbis. Rabbi Meir answered, 'From every part of the habitable world was the dust taken for the formation of Adam.' In a word, men of all lands and climes are brothers.

The Pentateuch and Haftorahs, Rabbi J H Hertz, ed.

HINDUISM AND RACIAL HARMONY

Hindus find it hard to be racist because of the persecution and discrimination they suffered when ruled by the Moghuls and the British. They also have something to offer to social harmony in the concept (rather than the practice) of caste. The caste system is based on interdependence and each part of society relying on the rest. Most modern Hindu groups, and most Hindus in the UK, reject caste but believe that the concept of caste and dharma means that we should treat all people equally and with respect.

The supreme example of Hindu attitudes to racism was Mohandas (Mahatma) Gandhi who fought for equal treatment of all races in South Africa and then led the campaign against British rule in India in which he encouraged all the different races and ethnic groups of India to live together as equals.

> When the central reality or God is all pervasive and religion creates no barriers between man and man then the denial of freedom and equality to all human beings is not only politically unjust but spiritually sinful.

The Harijan Journal.

> Every soul is potentially divine. Devotion to God should be by identifying the self with Brahman. In this way race and caste are transcended.

His Holiness Pramukh Swami Maharaj, Spiritual Leader of the Worldwide Bochasanwasi Shri Akshar Purushottam Swaminarayan Sanstha (BAPS).

BRITAIN AS A MULTI-FAITH SOCIETY

MULTI-FAITH SOCIETY – MANY DIFFERENT RELIGIONS IN ONE SOCIETY.

RELIGIOUS PLURALISM – ACCEPTING ALL FAITHS AS HAVING AN EQUAL RIGHT TO CO-EXIST.

Many societies were mono-faith (having only one religion) societies until the twentieth century.

In some ways, Great Britain has been a multi-faith society ever since the Reformation in the sixteenth century. Although Queen Elizabeth I made the Church of England the state religion, there were other churches: Protestants who were not Church of England (Non conformists), Roman Catholics, and from 1657 Jews. So Britain had to have laws encouraging religious toleration (everyone free to follow their chosen religion without discrimination).

The Huddersfield Gurdwara is located next door to the Salvation Army Citadel.

How Britain Legally Became a Religiously Plural Society

1671   Heresy ceased to be a crime.

1688   Nonconformists were given freedom of worship.

1828   Nonconformists were given the same political rights as members of the Church of England.

1829   Roman Catholics were given the same political rights as members of the Church of England.

1858   Jews were given the same political rights as members of the Church of England.

This meant that members of any religion were free to worship in Great Britain and had equal political rights.

However, it was in the twentieth century that Great Britain became truly multi-faith as members of non–Christian religions came to Britain as immigrants (although immigrants from the Caribbean and Africa were mainly Christian).

Religious Statistics for Great Britain

These statistics are based on *The UK Christian Handbook 1996/97*.

It is very difficult to compare statistics of membership of religions as some religions only count those who attend worship regularly whereas others count anyone born into the religion. These figures are based on the people who claimed some form of religious allegiance in 1994.

CHURCH OF ENGLAND	26.2 million		
NONCONFORMISTS	6.3 million		
ROMAN CATHOLIC	5.7 million		
Total number of Christian churches 49 847			
ISLAM	1.2 million	Mosques	800
JUDAISM	0.3 million	Synagogues	352
HINDUISM	0.4 million	Mandirs	144
SIKHISM	0.5 million	Gurdwaras	170
BUDDHISM	45 000	Monasteries etc.	213

Shri Swaminarayan Mandir, Neasden, opened in 1995.

The Tibetan Buddhist temple of Samye Ling in Dumfriesshire, opened in 1988.

All Christians believe in religious freedom, that is they believe everyone has the right to follow, or not follow, any religion they wish. However, there are different Christian attitudes to other religions:

1 Many Christians believe that in a multi-faith society, it is not fair to try to convert members of other faiths. They feel that all faiths must have some truth in them because of the good and holy lives they see Muslims, Hindus, Jews, Sikhs and Buddhists living in Britain today. So they feel that Christians should respect other faiths and work with other faiths to make Britain a more spiritual and holy country. They believe this not only because of the way Jesus did not try to convert the Jews, but also because they feel that the words of Jesus such as 'In my Father's house are many rooms' (John 14:2), mean that there is room in heaven for a variety of religions.

2 Other Christians feel that, although members of other faiths must be respected and given the freedom to practise their faith, everyone has the right to convert others. They believe they must try to convert everyone to Christianity because only Christians will go to heaven. They base their beliefs on sayings of Jesus such as, 'I am the way and the truth and the life. No-one comes to the Father except through me.' (John 14:6), and on the command of Jesus for people to love their neighbour. They feel that if you love your neighbour, you must want your neighbour to go to heaven and so you will want to convert them.

3 Many Christians, especially Roman Catholics, believe that non-Christian religions are searching for God and have some truth, but only Christianity has the whole truth. Only Christians worship God in a way of which he totally approves and so Christians have a right to try to convert people of other faiths.

This Chapel of Unity in Coventry Cathedral encourages Christians of different denominations and members of different faiths to join together.

FACTFILE 21

CHRISTIANITY AND OTHER RELIGIONS

All nations form but one community. This is so because all stem from the one stock which God created to people the entire earth, and also because all share a common destiny, namely God... The Catholic Church recognizes in other religions that search... for the God who is unknown yet near since he gives life and breath and all things.

Catechism of the Catholic Church.

The difference between Christianity and the other religions is not basically the difference between truth and error, but the difference between total and partial understanding.

Stephen Neill (Church of England bishop).

All religions have a common of faith in a higher reality which demands brotherhood on earth . . . Perhaps one day such names as Christianity, Buddhism, Islam, Hinduism will no longer be used to describe men's religious experience.

John Hick (Christian philosopher).

Christianity is the one true religion only because God decided so, only because the light of Christ falls on it . . . No matter how good and true any other religion might seem, it is false, useless – because the light of Christ has not fallen on it.

Karl Barth (Evangelical Protestant).

FACTFILE 22

ISLAM AND OTHER RELIGIONS

> **If anyone desires a religion other than Islam, never will it be accepted of him; and in the Hereafter, he will be in the ranks of those who have lost (all spiritual good).**

Surah 3:85

> **Nearest among them in love to the believers wilt thou find those who say 'we are Christians'.**

Surah 5:85

> **Let there be no compulsion in religion.**

Surah 2:256

Islam teaches that all people should have the freedom to worship in any way they wish, and that every individual has the right for their religious beliefs to be respected. The Qur'an clearly states that no one should be forced into believing or following a religion. The Qur'an also gives special mention and privileges to Jews and Christians.

On the other hand, Islam teaches that it is the only true religion; that Muhammad was given God's final and perfect revelation in the Qur'an and that Muslims have a duty to convert the whole world to Islam. The Qur'an says that only Muslims will go to heaven and so many Muslims feel they must try to convert others to Islam.

A small number of Muslims believe that there is truth in all religions and that each faith is just a different path to the same God. This is what the Persian poet, Rumi, meant when he said, 'The lamps are different, but the light is the same.'

> Although I am a Muslim, I think all religions should be treated the same. Everyone should have the right to follow their religion and live their life in their own way. We are all headed in the same direction, it is just our paths that are different.

Yasmeen Amehd, a Muslim student.

Christian visitors being welcomed into a mosque.

Jews have lived as a minority religion for 2000 years so they firmly believe in religious freedom and the right of people to worship the Almighty in any way they wish. They believe that if people follow other faiths, they can find God as long as they follow the teachings of the Ten Commandments as well.

This can be seen in the story of Jonah where the non-Jewish people of Nineveh were to be killed by God for their evil ways, but when they believed in God and changed their behaviour, God forgave them.

Jews believe that at the end of the world all religions will come together to worship God in the same way: 'But the Lord will rise upon you, and his glory will be seen upon you. And nations will come to your light, and kings to the brightness of your rising' (Isaiah 60:2-3).

Jews do not try to convert other faiths. People wanting to become Jews have to approach a synagogue. Jews work hard on inter-faith groups trying to promote good relations between religions. They object to those Christian groups who are trying to convert Jews to Christianity.

FACTFILE 23

JUDAISM AND OTHER RELIGIONS

> When God saw what they did and how they repented from their evil ways, God repented of the evil which he had said he would do to them, and he did not do it.

Jonah 3:10

Hinduism sees all religions as paths to the divine and sees religious toleration as a normal and essential part of life. There are so many different forms of Hinduism, with so many different ways of worshipping and so many different ways of looking at God that they can almost be regarded as separate religions within Hinduism. Hindus often take parts from other religions and make them a part of Hinduism. Indeed images of Jesus and the Buddha can be found in Hindu shrines.

> Religions are different roads converging to the same point. What does it matter that we take different roads as long as we reach the same goal? In reality, there are as many different religions as there are individuals.

Gandhi

FACTFILE 24

HINDUISM AND OTHER RELIGIONS

> All religions should stand side by side and go hand in hand. They are but one family... like windows in an endless tapestry of man's eternal search, they give visions of Truth and Reality. And the real truth of all religion is Harmony.

His Holiness Pramukh Swami Maharaj (BAPS).

RELIGIONS WORKING TOGETHER

The different Churches have worked together for many years. The Council of Churches for Britain and Ireland was established in 1990. It includes all the major Churches (there are 30 member Churches) and meets twice a year. England, Wales, Scotland and Ireland have their own groups which are organised in every town as 'Churches Together'.

The Council of Christians and Jews has existed since the Second World War to promote better understanding between the two religions and to prevent religious and racial bitterness.

The Inter-faith Network for the United Kingdom represents Buddhists, Christians, Hindus, Jains, Jews, Muslims and Sikhs. It works for increased tolerance and understanding and tries to encourage harmony by concentrating on what the religions have in common rather than on what divides them.

Many cities have their own groups to help the different religions in the city get along. In Glasgow, for example, the Sharing of Faiths movement was founded in the 1970's by Christians, Jews, Muslims, Sikhs and Hindus. It meets on a monthly basis and has an annual 'Presentation' in the city centre with stalls explaining each religion to the people of Glasgow. Its aim is sharing so that (without changing any of the religions) the people of Glasgow realise that each of these religions is a way of finding God and a purpose in life.

The Queen often meets with members of different religious communities.

Factfile 10 Social facts concerning the roles of men and women

1 Write down three pieces of evidence that women have gained more equality over the past 100 years.

2 Discuss in a group areas where women do not receive equal treatment and write down whether boys and girls have different views on this.

Factfile 11 Christianity and the roles of men and women

Divide a sheet of paper into two columns headed 'teachings that men and women have similar roles' and 'teachings that men and women have different roles'. Read through the factfile and fill in each column.

Factfiles 12, 13, 14 Islam, Judaism and Hinduism and the roles of men and women

Choose one religion and read through the factfile sorting out what the roles of men and women are, and next to each role write the reason given for that role.

Factfile 15 Social facts concerning the UK as a multi-ethnic society

Write down the following:
(a) two pieces of evidence that the UK has always been multi-ethnic;
(b) evidence that ethnic minorities are a very small proportion of the UK's population;
(c) the difference between prejudice and discrimination;
(d) what the law says about racial discrimination.

Factfile 16 Christianity and racial harmony

Write down two biblical and two Church reasons why Christianity is helping to achieve racial harmony.

Factfiles 17, 18, 19 Islam, Judaism, Hinduism and racial harmony

1 Choose one religion and write down how being a member of that religion would help you to achieve racial harmony.

2 'All religious people should fight against racism.'
Do you agree? Give reasons for your opinion, showing you have considered another point of view.

Factfile 20 Britain as a multi-faith society

1 What is the difference between a mono-faith and a religiously plural society?

2 How do religious laws in the UK show Britain is a multi-faith society?

Factfiles 21, 22, 23, 24, 25 Christianity, Islam, Judaism, Hinduism and other religions

1 Discuss with other members of your class what problems there might be for Christians and the members of one other religion in living in a multi-faith society.

2 'In a multi-faith society no religion should try to convert other people.'
Do you agree? Give reasons for your opinion, showing you have considered another point of view.

3 BELIEVING IN GOD

Introduction

This chapter is concerned with the reasons people have for believing, or not believing in God.

Some people may be led to believe in God for many reasons; others may believe for one reason and when they discover other reasons for believing in God, they find them helpful in supporting their belief in God.

There is no factfile on why people find it difficult to believe in God, you will have to discuss that, then receive a revision file from your teacher.

FACTFILE 26

RELIGIOUS UPBRINGING AND BELIEF IN GOD

If you were brought up as a Christian, you would learn about God from a very early age. You would be baptised and, to keep the promises they made at your baptism, your parents would probably teach you prayers as soon as you could talk.

Next you would go to Sunday School where you would learn more about God and how he made and looks after you. You would say prayers to God thanking him for looking after you and so it would seem natural to you to believe in God.

You would also be taken to church by your parents, especially at Christmas and Easter, and at church you would hear people talking about God and assuming that God exists.

All these teachings would be confirmed when you started school and there were assemblies, home-time prayers, and RE lessons when teachers referred to the things you had heard at home and at church.

> I am a Catholic because I was born to Catholic parents and I was educated in a Catholic school. All my upbringing made me believe in God and I have never really thought that God might not exist. God is a part of my life just as my parents and friends are.

A Catholic adult.

Confirmation ceremonies help children to believe in God.

If you were brought up as a Muslim, the very first words you would hear after your birth would be, 'Allah is great.' Your family would pray five times a day in the house and you would join in those prayers. At Ramadan the whole family would stop eating and drinking during daylight hours and this would make you aware that believing in God makes a difference to people's lives. You would be taken to a *madrasah* (a mosque school) as soon as you could talk properly and there you would be taught Arabic and learn the Qur'an as God's word. So it would seem natural to you to believe in God.

I have always believed in Allah. It was only when I was at secondary school that I realised there were people who did not believe in God. When you are brought up as a Muslim, you are aware of Allah's existence all the time.

A Muslim adult.

A madrasah (madrasa).

If you were brought up as a Jew, you would be aware of God from the very beginning as so many religious activities go on in the home. You would see your father putting on his tefillin and tallit to say his daily prayers; you would be involved every Friday in bringing in Sabbath with your mother and in the special prayers your father would say. At Pesach you would be involved in searching for leavened bread and finding out about what happened in the questions that the children are asked. You would go to lessons at the synagogue to find out about the Jewish faith, and you would be taken to synagogue services by your parents. In all these activities, you would find believing in God the most natural thing in the world.

I have always felt the Almighty around me. Home was full of reminders from the mezuzah on the doorposts to the way my mother prepared and cooked food. I was brought up in the Almighty's presence and never doubted it.

A Jewish adult.

Similarly if you were brought up as a Hindu, you would be aware of God from the beginning of your life. There would be a special naming ceremony and a ceremony for your first haircut, both of which would involve prayers to God. Your home would probably have a shrine and you would see the daily prayers and offerings made at the shrine. You would be taught to say mantras by your parents and you may well go to a Hindu Sunday school at your mandir. If you were a boy, you would go through your sacred thread ceremony when you were somewhere between 7 and 11 years of age. All of this upbringing would lead you to believe in God's existence.

Hindu children are brought up in their faith. These children are going to the Hindu Sunday School run at the Haveli Cultural Centre in Neasden.

FACTFILE 27

RELIGIOUS EXPERIENCE AND BELIEF IN GOD

Most people find that their religious upbringing leads them to believe in God and then their religious experience supports and confirms that belief. The Catholic Christian who said she was a Catholic because of her upbringing went on to say, 'All my experience of religion has convinced me that God exists. I know when I pray that God is listening to me. I feel at the Mass that Christ enters me.'

Religious experience can be defined in many ways, but the most common are:

- the feeling you get when you enter a great religious building or even a beautiful place, a feeling of awe and wonder, a feeling that there is something greater than you which you can only call God (a famous scholar, Rudolf Otto, called this 'the **numinous**');

- the feeling that there is something inside you wanting you to change your life and be more committed to your religion (some scholars call this **conversion** experience);

- a belief that a miracle has happened and that it must have been caused by God;

- a belief that your prayers have been answered (this is often connected to miracles e.g. if a Muslim prays for her mother to be cured of cancer and she is, she will believe both that her prayers have been answered and that God has caused a miracle to happen – both of which will lead her to believe that God exists);

- an experience where you feel that you have been in contact with God in a special way (this is often called '**mystical**' and can range from a very strong numinous experience to going into trances, having visions etc.).

Followers of all religions have experiences like these which lead them to believe that God must exist. The files of the Religious Experience Research Unit contain thousands of accounts of people who believe they have had religious experiences.

> My daughter, Joan, was killed by a car when she was seven years old. She and I were very close and I was grief stricken. She was lying in her coffin in her bedroom, I fell on my knees by the bedside. Suddenly I felt as if something a bit behind me was so overcome with pity that it was consolidating itself. Then I felt a touch on my shoulder lasting only an instant, and I knew there was another world.

A numinous experience.

Incident from the files of the Religious Experience Research Unit published in *The Spiritual Nature of Man*, Sir Alister Hardy.

> At one time I reached utter despair and went and prayed God for mercy, instinctively and without faith in reply. That night I stood with other patients in the grounds waiting to be let into our ward. It was a very cold night with many stars. Suddenly someone stood beside me in a dusty brown robe and a voice said, 'Mad or sane you are one of My sheep'. I never spoke to anyone of this, but ever since it has been a pivot of my life.

A mystical experience.

Incident from the files of the Religious Experience Research Unit.

> Towards the end of Ramadan in his fortieth year, when he was alone in the cave, there came to him an angel in the form of a man. The Angel said to him, 'Recite!' and he said: 'I am not a reciter', whereupon, as he himself told it, 'the Angel took me and whelmed me in his embrace until he had reached the limit of mine endurance he released me and said: 'Recite!', and again I said, 'I am not a reciter.' Then a third time he whelmed me as before, then released me and said:
> 'Recite in the name of thy Lord who created!
>   He created man from a clot of blood.
> Recite; and thy Lord is the Most Bountiful,
> He who hath taught by the pen,
> Taught man what he knew not.'
> He recited these words after the Angel, who thereupon left him; and he said, 'It was as though the words were written on my heart.'

The call of Muhammad recorded in *Muhammad his life based on the earliest sources*, M Lings.

The Cave Hira, near Mecca (Makkah), where Muhammad had his visit from the Angel.

We had a speaker, Colin Urquart, who said something that made me realise that all this time (Carol had been searching for God) my problem had been that I hadn't accepted that God had accepted me. I now knew that God had accepted me, and I felt reassured that what I had been searching for all these years I actually had anyway. I felt a sort of freedom and confidence in knowing that God was real to me and real in my life. That was the turning point.

Carol Mason's conversion experience as recorded in *Christians in Britain Today*.

Miracles

Most religious people believe in miracles.

By 'a miracle', they usually mean 'an event which seems to break a natural law and for which the only explanation is God'.

Some religious people think that a miracle is 'a natural event which must be caused by God because of the time at which it occurs and the religious connections it has'. Such a miracle would be the English Channel staying calm so that British troops could be evacuated from Dunkirk in 1940.

In August 1879, an image of the Virgin Mary, along with St Joseph and St John the Evangelist, appeared on the outside wall of the Catholic church in the Irish village of Knock. It was seen by at least 15 different villagers who all stated that: it was very bright; it reached almost to the ground; when they tried to touch the figures, all they could feel was the wall. It could not have been a projection because, when the villagers stood in front of the figures, they cast no shadows on the wall.

They could think of no explanation except that this was a miracle and it made some of them go back to believing in God because, if he can make a miracle happen, he must exist.

In the same way in the gospels, when Jesus healed lepers, gave sight to the blind and raised the dead, people began to believe in God because there seemed to be no other explanation for what had happened.

Many religious believers think that miracles still happen today. Quite often at Christian healing services, people suffering from incurable cancers are healed. They, and the people who have prayed for them, believe they have been healed by God performing a miracle.

If miracles happen, then they are obviously a reason for believing in God, because God must exist if they happen!

The Shrine at Knock – a place of pilgrimage and healing.

Many people look at the world, the solar system, the universe and feel that it all appears to be designed:

EXPERIENCE OF THE WORLD AND BELIEF IN GOD

- the way DNA are so carefully structured that a tiny fertilised human egg (almost invisible to the naked eye) is the blueprint for an adult human being;

- the way in which the Big Bang (the cosmic explosion which many scientists believe was the beginning of the universe) was so designed – the size and timing of the explosion, the laws of gravity and the nature of matter – that human life was bound to evolve;

- all this implies that there is design in the universe and if there is design, there must be a designer, and who could that be but God?

> If you came across a watch in an uninhabited place, you could not say it had been put there by chance. The complexity of its mechanism would make you say it had a designer. The universe is far more complex than a watch and so if a watch needs a watchmaker, the universe needs a universe maker and that could only be God.

Abridged from *Natural Theology,* William Paley.

A spiral galaxy forming in the aftermath of the Big Bang (computer artwork).

Other people look at the world and see that everything seems to have a cause. If everything has a cause, then it is logical to assume that the universe has a cause and that could only be God.

Science is based on the idea that everything has an explanation, things do not 'just happen'. If everything in the universe has an explanation, it is reasonable to believe that the universe itself needs an explanation, and the only possible explanation of the universe is God.

Other people find that their whole experience of life makes them believe that life has a purpose. Birth, marriage, careers, the way we need to love people and be loved by people make them feel that they can't be here by chance. There must be a reason for them being here – life must have a purpose. It is in looking for a purpose in life that many people turn to religion and are led to believe in God.

Many people experience life as a cycle in which everything depends on everything else, like the Nitrogen Cycle.

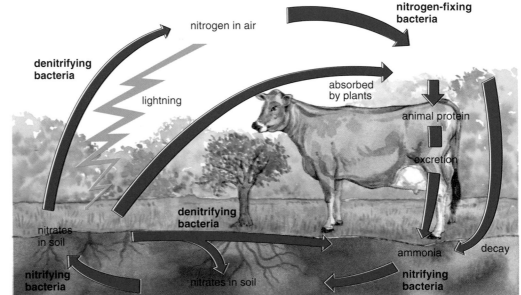

Our prayers may differ in words and ways, but they convey the same feelings!
Our pilgrim places may differ in place and form, but they carry the same sanctity!
Our morals may differ in phrase and style, but they preach the same message!
Our religions may differ in symbols and names, but they reveal the same meaning – universal harmony.

His Holiness Pramukh Swami Maharaj (BAPS).

Some people think that religion itself is evidence for God's existence. People have always had religious beliefs – the Stone Age cave paintings all depict forms of religion. There are also many similarities in religion:

• The idea of God as creator.

• The belief that it is possible to get in touch with God.

• The moral rules of religions.

• The miracles and visions which occur in all religions.

• Prayer.

It may be that, just as the laws of science were there waiting to be discovered by scientists, so God is there waiting to be discovered by religion.

MORAL EVIL – SUFFERING WHICH IS CAUSED BY HUMAN BEINGS DOING WRONG THINGS AS IN THE BEER BOTTLE EXAMPLE.

NON-MORAL/NATURAL EVIL – SUFFERING WHICH IS CAUSED BY THE WAY THINGS ARE IN THE WORLD E.G. THE SUFFERING CAUSED BY AN EARTHQUAKE.

BENEVOLENT – GOOD/KIND.

OMNISCIENT – ALL-KNOWING.

OMNIPOTENT – ALL-POWERFUL.

THEODICY – A WAY OF EXPLAINING WHY THERE IS SUFFERING IN A WORLD MADE BY A GOOD ALL-POWERFUL GOD.

THE PROBLEM OF EVIL AND SUFFERING

Evil and suffering are linked together because evil is wrong, and most people think it is wrong for people to suffer. Usually, evil also causes suffering, e.g. if I do wrong by attacking you with a beer bottle, my evil actions will cause you suffering.

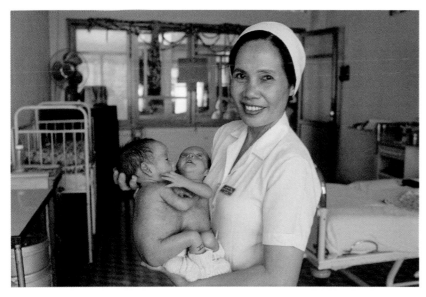

Could a good God create Siamese twins?

The problem of evil and suffering

Evil and suffering cause problems for religious believers because:

- If God is good, he must want to get rid of suffering.

- If God is all-knowing, he must have known what suffering would result from creating the world.

- If God is all-powerful, he must be able to prevent or get rid of suffering.

As there is suffering in the world, it would appear that God cannot be good and all-knowing and all-powerful.

As most religious believers believe that God is all-knowing, all-powerful and good, this is bound to cause them a problem.

CHRISTIAN RESPONSES TO EVIL AND SUFFERING

There are many different ways in which Christians respond to suffering. Some are practical, others are more theoretical and many Christians would combine the two.

The main response of Christians to suffering is a practical one – to help those who are suffering.

This is done either by:

- PRAYER (asking God to help those who are suffering – such prayer is called intercession and is a feature of nearly every Christian act of worship)

or by

- SERVICE (actively helping those who suffer) – many Christians help in hospitals and hospices, organise food and clothing for down and outs in Great Britain, raise money to help less developed countries etc. This is often done in response to Jesus' advice in the parable of the Sheep and the Goats.

The parable of the Sheep and the Goats:

> **Then the righteous will answer him, 'Lord when did we see you hungry and feed you, or thirsty and give you something to drink? When did we see you a stranger and invite you in, or needing clothes and clothe you? When did we see you sick or in prison and go to visit you?' The King will reply, 'I tell you the truth, whatever you did for one of the least of these my brothers, you did for me.'**

Matthew 25:37–40

Christians believe that the suffering of Jesus shows that God cares about our sufferings. (*Crucifixion* by Xavier Jones.)

- Many Christians connect the idea of **free will** with evil and suffering. According to Genesis 1, God created us in his image which means he created us with free will. He wants us to be free people who decide for ourselves whether to believe in God or not. To be free means free to do either good or evil, and so God could not have created free people who always did the good. Evil and suffering are caused by human misuse of free will and so are not the fault of God.

- Other Christians point out that this world was not created as a paradise. God created this world as **a preparation for paradise**. Paradise comes after we die in heaven. So in this world we have to live in such a way that we improve our souls and become good enough to enter paradise. These Christians also believe that to do good requires evil – I cannot share my wealth if there are no poor people. So God made this world with the possibility of evil, but in the next world there will be no evil or suffering.

- Many Christians believe there is no point in worrying about the problem because **we cannot understand God's reasons** for doing things. God must have a reason for allowing evil and suffering, but there is no way we can know what it is because we are not God. However, we do know from the life of Jesus that even God's own Son had to suffer, and that Jesus commanded his followers to respond to suffering by helping those who suffer. Jesus healed the sick, fed the hungry and even raised the dead, and we should respond in the same way – by helping to remove suffering.

> Then I saw a new heaven and a new earth for the first heaven and the first earth had passed away... Now the dwelling of God is with men, and he will live with them. They will be his people, and God himself will be with them and be their God. He will wipe every tear from their eyes. There will be no more death or mourning or crying or pain.'

Revelation 21:1-4

The shrine at Lourdes is visited by thousands of suffering Christians, some of whom believe that they are cured by God.

ISLAMIC RESPONSES TO EVIL AND SUFFERING

> **And behold We said to the angels: 'Bow down to Adam' and they bowed down. Not so Iblis: he refused and was haughty: he was of those who reject the faith.**

Surah 2:34

> **Be sure We shall test you with something of fear and hunger, some loss in goods or lives or the fruits of your toil, but give glad tidings to those who patiently persevere – who say when afflicted with calamity, 'To God we belong and to Him is our return.'**

Surah 2:155-6

Islam believes that evil and suffering are a test from God.

When God created the earth and made Adam to look after it, he asked the angels to bow down to Adam as his vice-regent (humans are superior to angels as they have free will – which is why they can be vice-regents – but they are inferior because their free will means they can sin). Satan (Iblis) refused to bow down, and was thrown out of heaven. However, God allowed Satan to use evil to tempt humans to reject Islam. When the Last Day arrives, Satan will be sent to hell to be punished. So Muslims believe that suffering and evil are a test from God. If people's faith in Islam remains strong, they will be rewarded by God with eternity in heaven.

Muslims believe that the way to pass the test of suffering, such as these floods in Bangladesh, is to help those who suffer, often through groups like Muslim Aid.

JEWISH RESPONSES TO EVIL AND SUFFERING

> Not to have known suffering is not to be truly human.

Midrash

The Jewish philosopher Maimonides taught that God created people free, to worship him or not worship him. However, if God gave people only good things, then they would lose that freedom because having only good things would force them to worship God. So God gives both bad and good things to keep people free.

The Holocaust (the name given to the Nazis' attempt to wipe out all the Jews of Europe during the Second World War) has had a tremendous impact on Jewish attitudes to evil and suffering. Why did God allow his chosen people to suffer so much through no fault of their own? Many answers have been given based on the answers given in the Jewish Bible, but the main response has been to regard it as a call for the Jews to overcome suffering in the world.

Nowadays, most Jews believe that we should accept suffering when it happens to us, but relieve suffering when it happens to others, 'Regard the needy as members of your household', *Ethics of the Fathers*.

So there are many Jewish care agencies in Great Britain running housing schemes and day centres for the elderly, disabled and blind. Norwood Child Care provides help for families suffering from poverty, disability and marriage breakdown.

The Jewish Bible says many different things about suffering:

- It is a punishment from God

> **It is not because of your righteousness... that you are going to take possession of their land; but on account of the wickedness of these nations, that the Lord is going to drive them out before you.**

Deuteronomy 9:5

> **Blessed is the man whom God corrects: so do not despise the discipline of the Almighty.**

Job 5:17

- It is a test from God

> **Some time later God tested Abraham...**

Genesis 22:1

- It is a way of bringing people to God

> **He was despised and rejected by men, a man of sorrows and familiar with suffering... Yet it was the Lord's will to crush him and cause him to suffer, and though the Lord makes his life a guilt-offering, he will see his offspring and prolong his days.**

Isaiah 53:3,10

> Because of Auschwitz I therefore identify with those many people throughout the world who have suffered, and who suffer, from a discrimination which rejects them because of differences, because of their creed or the colour of their skin or of their hair, or the shape of their nose.

The watchtowers of Auschwitz are a permanent reminder of the crimes carried out by the Nazis.

I am a Jew, Moshe Davis.

FACTFILE 33

HINDU RESPONSES TO EVIL AND SUFFERING

> Great souls who have become one with Me have reached the highest good. They do not undergo rebirth, a condition which is impermanent and full of pain and suffering.
>
> *Bhagavad Gita 8:15*

Hindus believe that suffering is an essential part of samsara (the cycle of lives), so suffering is a natural part of life. People are born in suffering and die in suffering until they attain moksha which can be regarded as release from suffering.

Hindus follow the law of karma – whatever evil people do in this life will be paid back in the way they are reborn – so they believe that human beings are the main reason for the existence of evil and suffering in the world. Anything that people suffer in this life is because of their karma – people cause their own suffering by their behaviour in previous lives.

Some Hindus, therefore, fail to respond to the suffering around them. They see it as the fault of the people who suffer and if they prevent their suffering, those people will just have to suffer again in a future life.

The majority of Hindus feel that it is their dharma (duty) to help those who suffer. Gandhi refused to accept that the outcastes were suffering because of karma. He called them the *Harijan* (Children of God) and tried to relieve their suffering as a way of improving his own karma – the Indian government gave outcastes equal treatment under the law as soon as India became independent.

Cremation releases the soul from suffering.

Factfile 27 Religious experience and belief in God

1 Define two types of religious experience.

2 Describe a religious experience.

3 Explain how having a religious experience might make someone believe in God.

Factfile 28 Experience of the world and belief in God

1 Divide a page into two columns headed 'Believe in God' and 'Not believe in God'. Then go through people's experiences of the world and put them into one of the columns. You will need to think about what goes into the second column, as this is not given in the book!

2 'The world has been designed by God.' Do you agree? Give reasons for your answer, showing you have considered another point of view.

Factfile 29 The problem of evil and suffering

Write down in your own words why the fact that evil and suffering exist in the world makes it difficult to believe in God.

Factfiles 30, 31, 32, 33 Christian, Islamic, Jewish and Hindu responses to evil and suffering

1 Write down one response to the problem of evil and suffering from Christianity and one from one of the other religions.

2 Discuss in a group whether these responses succeed in dealing with the problem.

3 'Miracles don't happen today.' Do you agree? Give reasons for your answer, showing that you have considered other points of view.

THE SANCTITY OF LIFE

The beliefs of all religions on the sanctity of life tend to be contained in their attitudes to life after death, abortion and euthanasia. However, it is possible to see some specific teaching on the sanctity (holiness, sacredness) of life.

All religions believe that life is a gift from God and so essentially belongs to God.

> **You shall not murder.**

Exodus 20:13 (the sixth Commandment)

> **Do you not know that your body is a temple of the Holy Spirit, who is in you, whom you have received from God? You are not your own.**

1 Corinthians 6:19

Christian Teachings

Christians believe life is a gift from God and therefore it is sacred. Regarding life as sacred means it is to be treated as holy and therefore valued and preserved.

Christians believe that because life is created by God, life has a special relationship with God. God is always a part of life and humans do not have the right to do what they like with human life. Christians believe that the human body belongs to its creator, God, and so life and death decisions must be in God's hands.

The sacredness of life is seen especially by Christians in the life and death of Jesus. They believe that God sanctified human life by becoming human, and that the way Jesus suffered without attempting to do anything to cut short his sufferings, shows that life is not to be ended except when God decides.

Muslim Teachings

> **Nor can a soul die except by God's leave, the term being fixed as by writing.**

Surah 3:145

Islam teaches that God alone is the author (creator) of life and so all life is sacred to God. This means that life itself is holy and so, in Islam, any aggression against human life is an attack on God. It is the second great sin in Islam, second only to associating other beings with God.

Islam teaches that it is God alone who grants life or death and so humans have no right to interfere with this. Life comes from God and belongs to God and so it is holy.

Jewish Teachings

Jews base their beliefs on the teachings of the Tenakh, that life is a gift from God. As God is the author of life, it follows that life must be sacred. It is holy and must be valued and preserved.

Jews believe that God is in control of his creation and that whatever comes to life or dies is caused to do so by God. Humans therefore have to respect all human life and they have no right to interfere with it, as it is up to God to say when life will begin or end.

> Naked I came from my mother's womb, and naked I shall depart. The Lord gave and the Lord has taken away; may the name of the Lord be praised.

Job 1:21

Hindu Teachings

Hindus believe that all life is sacred because all souls are immortal. The souls of all living creatures are one and the same as the eternal Brahman; therefore to take life is to hurt Brahman.

The Hindu belief in the sacredness of life is connected with the idea that God is in everything and so to respect all life is to respect God.

> This joy supreme comes to the Yogi whose heart is still, whose passions are at peace, who is pure from sin, who is one with Brahman, with God. He sees himself in the heart of all beings and he sees all beings in his heart. This is the vision of the Yogi of harmony, a vision which is of oneness. He who in this oneness of love, loves me in whatever he sees, wherever this man may live, in truth this man lives in me.

Bhagavad Gita 6:27-31

New life is seen by religious people as a gift from God.

CHRISTIAN TEACHING ON LIFE AFTER DEATH

Christians have two basic concepts about life after death:

RESURRECTION – AFTER DEATH NOTHING HAPPENS, BUT AT A TIME IN THE FUTURE (OFTEN CALLED THE LAST DAY OR THE DAY OF JUDGEMENT) THE DEAD WILL BE BROUGHT BACK TO LIFE (RAISED) AND BE GIVEN AN IMMORTAL (ETERNAL) BODY.

IMMORTALITY OF THE SOUL – THE BELIEF THAT HUMANS HAVE A BODY AND A SOUL (PERSONALITY, SELF) WHICH SURVIVES DEATH AND AFTER DEATH GOES TO A SPIRITUAL (NON-PHYSICAL) PLACE WHERE GOD IS.

> I look for the resurrection of the dead and the life of the world to come.

Nicene Creed

> I believe in... the resurrection of the body and the life everlasting.

Apostle's Creed

Christ has indeed been raised from the dead, the first fruits of those who have fallen asleep. For since death came through a man, the resurrection of the dead comes also through a man. For as in Adam all men die, so in Christ all will be made alive... But someone may ask, 'How are the dead raised? With what kind of body will they come?' How foolish! What you sow does not come to life unless it dies. When you sow, you do not plant the body that will be, but just a seed, perhaps of wheat or something else. But God gives it a body as he has determined... So it will be with the resurrection of the dead. The body that is sown perishable, it is raised imperishable; it is sown in dishonour, it is raised in glory; it is sown in weakness, it is raised in power; it is sown in a natural body, it is raised a spiritual body.

1 Corinthians 15:20-22,35-38,42-44

Then he (the criminal crucified with Jesus) said, 'Jesus, remember me when you come into your kingdom.' Jesus answered him, 'I tell you the truth, today you will be with me in paradise.'

Luke 23:42.43

Christians believe that faith in Jesus can overcome death and evil, which is the theme of this Baptistry window in Coventry Cathedral.

Christians have different views about the nature of life after death depending on whether they believe in resurrection or immortality.

1 Many Evangelical Protestants believe in the resurrection of the body as outlined in 1 *Corinthians* 15. They believe that when people die, their soul waits until the time when God will end the world (the Last Day before which Jesus will return to the earth). Then the dead will be raised and will join the living in the presence of God. Those who have been dead for a time will not be aware of any passage of time between their death and the Last Day.

On the Last Day everyone will come before God to be judged. The judgement will be based on Christian faith and behaviour. Good Christians will then go to heaven for eternity, whilst Christians who have sinned and not repented, and non-Christians will go to hell for eternity.

These beliefs are based on the teachings of St Paul and the resurrection of Jesus whose body was raised from the dead.

2 Many Protestants believe in the immortality of the soul. They believe that when people die, their soul lives on in a spiritual realm. They believe that souls go immediately before God to be judged and that good Christians will go to heaven. Some believe that bad Christians and non-Christians will go to hell. However, many of these Christians do not believe in hell, they believe that there will be an after-life for all people and all religions, but what happens to people in that after-life will be affected by how they have lived this life.

These beliefs are based on Jesus saying to the thief that he would be in heaven on Good Friday (Luke 23:43); Jesus' statement about the many rooms in his father's house (John 14:2); the belief in the communion of saints (that there can be communication between living and dead Christians) and the evidence of parapsychology (things like ghosts, mediums, telepathy).

3 Roman Catholics believe in both resurrection and immortality. They believe that at death: the souls of those who have not sinned since their last confession will go straight to heaven; the souls of Christians who have sinned will go to purgatory for their souls to be cleansed; the souls of those who have refused to believe in God or who have committed mortal sins (a deliberate very evil act which has not been repented of) will go to hell.

Then Jesus will come back to Earth, the dead will be raised and the souls will be reunited with their bodies. Then God will judge everyone. God will make a new heaven and a new earth, the souls who are in heaven or purgatory will go to heaven and the souls in hell will return to hell.

These beliefs are based on the resurrection of Jesus, the teachings of the New Testament and the teachings of the Church. They are stated in the new Catholic Catechism.

> **In my Father's house there are many rooms; if it were not so I would have told you. I am going there to prepare a place for you.**
>
> *John 14:2*

> **Then I saw a great white throne and him who was seated on it. Earth and sky fled from his presence, and there was no place for them. And I saw the dead, great and small, standing before the throne and books were opened... The dead were judged according to what they had done as recorded in the books... Then death and hades were thrown into the lake of fire. The lake of fire is the second death. If anyone's name was not found written in the book of life, he was thrown into the lake of fire. Then I saw a new heaven and a new earth, for the first heaven and the first earth had passed away, and there was no longer any sea. I saw the Holy City, the new Jerusalem, coming down out of heaven from God.**
>
> *Revelation 20:11-15, 21:1-2*

> Christians differ in their views about life after death. But they all believe that this life has a meaning and purpose, and that it is sacred and should not be destroyed by anyone.

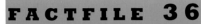

MUSLIM TEACHING ON LIFE AFTER DEATH

> On the Day of Judgement, the whole of the earth will be but His handful and the heavens will be rolled up in His right hand... The trumpet will be sounded when all that are in the heavens and the earth will swoon (lose consciousness) except such as it will please God to exempt. Then will a second one be sounded, when, behold, they will be standing and looking on! And the earth will shine with the glory of its Lord.

Surah 39:67-69

> That Day shall all men be sorted out. Then those who have believed and worked righteous deeds shall be made happy in a mead of delight. And those who have rejected faith and falsely denied Our signs and the meeting of the Hereafter – such shall be brought forth to punishment.

Surah 30:14-16

The Muslim view on life after death is that this life is given by God as a test. So it has meaning and purpose and should not be destroyed.

Muslims do not believe in the immortality of the soul. They believe that when people die, their body stays in the grave until the Last Day. On the Last Day everything will be destroyed and everyone will die. Then God will raise everyone from death so that bodies will be raised. Everyone will be gathered before God and judged on the basis of whether they have lived their lives as good Muslims following the way of life given by God in the Qur'an and the Shari'ah.

Muslims believe that those who pass the Final Judgement will go to heaven for eternity and those who fail will go to hell for eternity. However, Muslims also believe that God is compassionate and forgiving – 'Whoever does evil will be requited accordingly nor will he find, besides God, any protector or helper' (Surah 4:123) – and so they believe God will forgive faithful Muslims who have tried their best, but sinned.

Most Muslims believe that non-Muslims will go to hell, but some believe that God will forgive non-Muslims who have lived good lives.

Because of their beliefs about resurrection, Muslims are never cremated and do not remove any of the contents of the body at death. Many Muslims visit family graves at religious festival times and seem to believe that the souls of the dead remain at the grave until the Last Day.

Muslims live their lives always aware that all that they do is being noted and they will be judged on it at the Last Day.

Graves of holy men (*pirs*) are specially looked after in Pakistan.

Jews have similar teaching on life after death to Muslims and Christians.

1 Many Jews believe in the resurrection of the dead, indeed it is one of the Thirteen Principles of the Faith set out by Maimonides which all Jews are expected to believe. They believe that God will end this world when he decides to do so. Then he will create a new world and resurrect the dead. He will rebuild the city of Jerusalem and the Temple and good Jews will live there for eternity. These beliefs are based on the teachings of the Tenakh and the Talmud and the Thirteen Principles.

2 Some Jews believe that there is a spirit world into which all souls will go immediately after death. They believe that God would not allow death to be the end, and cannot accept the idea of the Last Day and recreation of the Earth.

All Jews believe that what happens to people when they die is determined by how they have lived this life. So Jews are expected to make a death-bed confession if possible and there is a special prayer in the Jewish Prayer Book for people to say if they know they are dying.

Jewish cemeteries are called the House of Life symbolising the Jewish belief that death is not the end and that the Almighty will look after his faithful servants beyond the grave.

The Jewish Cemetery in Prague.

JEWISH TEACHING ON LIFE AFTER DEATH

I believe with perfect faith that there will be a resurrection of the dead at a time when it will please the Creator, blessed be his name, and exalted be the remembrance of him for ever and ever.

Number 13 of the *Thirteen Principles of Faith.*

O Lord of compassion remember unto him (her) for good all the meritorious and pious deeds which he (she) wrought while on earth. Open unto him (her) the gates of righteousness and light, the gates of pity and grace. O shelter him (her) for evermore under the cover of thy wings; and let his (her) soul be bound up in the bond of eternal life.

Prayer for home service prior to a funeral, *The Authorised Daily Prayer Book.*

This world is like an antechamber to the world to come; prepare thyself in the antechamber that thou mayest enter into the hall.

Mishnah

Jewish belief in life after death gives life meaning and purpose. A Jew knows that if they worship God and follow his laws in their life, then God will reward them.

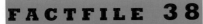

FACTFILE 38

HINDU TEACHING ON LIFE AFTER DEATH

> **Finite they say are these our bodies indwelt by an eternal embodied soul – a soul indestructible... As a man casts off his worn out clothes and takes on other new ones in their place, so does the embodied soul cast off his worn out bodies and enters others anew... For sure is the death of all that comes to birth, sure the birth of all that dies.**

Bhagavad Gita 2:18,22,27

> **From the unreal lead me to the real, from darkness lead me to light, from death lead me to immortality.**

Brihadaranyaka Upanishad 1:3.28

Hindu beliefs about life after death are quite different from Christianity, Judaism and Islam. Hindus believe in the immortality of the soul (atman) which can never be destroyed. However, they believe that after death, every soul is reborn into another body. This belief is called reincarnation or transmigration, and this process of rebirth will continue until the soul gains release from rebirth.

The release from rebirth (moksha) happens in different ways for different Hindus. Most Hindus believe that it happens over a long period of time by people fulfilling their duty (dharma). If this is done in every rebirth, then eventually they will become a sannyasin and instead of being reborn will reach moksha, a state of bliss free from sorrow and free from desire.

This state of bliss is sometimes called nirvana, or ananda, and is thought of in different ways. Some Hindus think of it as the merging of the soul with Brahman in the same way that a drop of water reunites with the ocean. Others think of the soul becoming one with God but still keeping its own identity. Others think of it as heaven where the soul is like one of the gods and lives with them.

There are also many different Hindu ideas on how to reach moksha apart from following your dharma. Some think it can come in one life through devotion to God or through meditation. Others think that knowledge of the nature of God will give moksha.

Whatever their views, Hindus try to live their lives avoiding evil things, fulfilling their duty in their ashrama (stage of life) and trying to make spiritual progress.

His Holiness Pramukh Swami Maharaj, Spiritual Leader of BAPS.

Hindu beliefs in life after death mean that life has purpose and meaning and is sacred.

ABORTION – THE TERMINATION OF THE LIFE OF A FOETUS

INFANTICIDE – KILLING A BABY AFTER BIRTH

ABORTION ON DEMAND – WOMEN BEING ALLOWED AN ABORTION WITHOUT ANY QUESTIONS ASKED.

SOCIAL FACTS ON ABORTION

Table of abortions carried out in England and Wales

1971	1991	1993	1995
104 000	190 000	180 000	116 000
22% on women more than 12 weeks pregnant		12% on women more than 12 weeks pregnant	

Source: Social Trends 28.

The 1967 Act states that an abortion can be carried out if two doctors agree that:

- the mother's life is at risk;

- there is a risk of injury to the mother's physical or mental health;

- there is a risk that another child would put at risk the mental or physical health of existing children;

- there is a substantial risk that the baby might be born seriously handicapped.

Until 1967 all abortions in Great Britain were illegal, but this did not mean they did not happen. There were thousands of 'backstreet abortions' where desperate women paid unqualified people for an abortion and often died as a result. This is the main argument put forward by those who believe in abortion. They claim that it is impossible to get rid of abortions because if women do not want a child, they will try every possible method to get rid of it. The country with the largest number of abortions and the largest number of deaths from abortion is Brazil where abortion is illegal.

Abortions in Great Britain were made legal by the 1967 Abortion Act which was amended in 1990. The 1990 Act states that abortions cannot take place after 24 weeks of pregnancy unless the mother's life is at risk because advances in medical techniques mean that such foetuses have a slim chance of survival.

The crucial issue for much discussion about abortion is, 'When does life begin?'

- **One view is that life begins at conception.**
  Many religions and anti-abortion groups such as Life believe that life begins as soon as the male sperm and female ovum combine.

- **Another view is that life begins at some definite point during pregnancy.**
  Some people think that life does not begin until the baby starts to move in the womb. Thomas Aquinas, a medieval philosopher, believed that a foetus becomes a human being when God implants the soul (he thought this was 40 days after conception for boys and 90 days for girls). People in many religions believe that there is a point in pregnancy where God implants the soul so that the foetus becomes a sacred life.

The **'doctrine of double effect'** is often used in discussing both abortion and euthanasia. This is the idea that if a person takes an action to attain one effect knowing that it will produce another, they cannot be blamed for the second effect occurring. For example, if a person removes a cancerous tumour from the womb of a pregnant woman they know this will kill the foetus, but this is not an abortion, because their intention is simply to remove the cancer.

- **A third view is that life begins when a baby is capable of living outside the womb.**
  Many people believe that a baby cannot be considered as a separate life until it is capable of living outside its mother. Until then it is part of the mother. Professor JJ Thomson argues that a foetus does not have a right to be kept in a mother's body, any more than someone who needs a rare blood type if they are not to die has the right to take blood from a person with a similar blood type. Unless a woman tries to get pregnant, the foetus has no claims on her.

Many anti-abortion campaigns are led by Christians.

FACTFILE 40

CHRISTIANITY AND ABORTION

> **Before I formed you in the womb I knew you, before you were born I set you apart.**
>
> *Jeremiah 1:5*

1 Roman Catholics and most Evangelical Protestants think that all forms of abortion are sinful and should not be allowed. They are the main organisers of groups such as LIFE and SPUC (Society for the Unborn Child) which campaign for the rights of the foetus.

They base their beliefs on certain Christian teachings:

- the sanctity of life and the belief that all life is holy and belongs to God, therefore only God has the right to end a pregnancy;

- the belief that life begins at the moment of conception;

- the belief that the unborn child is created in the image of God and is one for whom Jesus, the Son of God died;

- the belief that every human being has a right to life.

2 Other Protestants such as the Church of England and the Methodist Church agree that abortion is an evil, but feel that sometimes the lesser of two evils has to be chosen and that Christians should always do what is the most loving thing in the circumstances. They would allow abortion if the pregnancy was a result of rape, because it would be necessary to allow an innocent person to recover. They would also allow abortion where the embryo is handicapped so that birth would only give a life of great suffering or early death. They would allow abortion where the life of the mother is threatened. Some would also allow abortion for social reasons such as poverty and the effects on the rest of the family.

Such Christians base their attitude on the following Christian teachings:

- Jesus told Christians to love their neighbour as themselves and abortion may be the most loving thing.

- Christians have to face up to new technology and accept the advances in medicine to cure illness. They should accept advances such as amniocentesis (tests in early pregnancy to predict certain handicaps in the foetus) to prevent disease and suffering.

- Christianity is concerned with justice and it would be unjust to ban abortions because it would affect the poor more than the rich (the rich would still be able to buy abortions).

- The sanctity of life can be broken in such things as war when people are killed, so there could be justification for abortion.

- Life does not begin at conception.

Islam does not allow abortion 'after the foetus is completely formed and has been given a soul' (*The Lawful and the Prohibited in Islam*). However, this allows a variety of attitudes to abortion among Muslims.

1 The majority of Muslims believe that abortion is a great sin, but may be allowed if the life of the mother is threatened. They base this attitude on the teachings of Islam about the sanctity of life, especially the Islamic view that all life belongs to God alone. There are also teachings in the Qur'an which say that children should not be killed. The Shari'ah says that where there is a choice between the life of the mother and the life of the child, the mother's life always takes priority. This is based on the lesser of two evils, in that the loss of the mother's life would cause so much family disruption. This does not mean that they regard abortion as right, simply that where a death is unavoidable the death of the unborn child is a lesser evil.

2 Some Muslims believe that abortion cannot be permitted at any time at all. They base their attitude on the belief that the soul is given at the moment of conception and on the teachings of the Qur'an against abortion.

3 Some Muslims accept that abortion is permitted up to 120 days of the pregnancy, but that there must be good reasons such as the health of the mother or the health of the future baby. They would therefore allow an abortion if tests showed the foetus was abnormal. They base this attitude on the teachings of some Muslim lawyers that the embryo is unformed and soulless up to 120 days old. They believe that the teachings of Islam opposing abortion only come into effect after the foetus is completely formed and has been given a soul and that does not happen until 120 days of pregnancy.

> **Dear friends let us love one another, for love comes from God. Everyone who loves has been born of God and knows God. Whoever does not love does not know God, because God is love.**
>
> *1 John 4:7–8*

FACTFILE 41

ISLAM AND ABORTION

> **Kill not your children on a plea of want. We provide sustenance for you and for them; Come not nigh to shameful deeds.**
>
> *Surah 6:151*

> **Kill not your children for fear of want: we shall provide sustenance for them as well as for you. Verily the killing of them is a great sin.**
>
> *Surah 17:31*

FACTFILE 42

JUDAISM AND ABORTION

> **See now that I myself am He! There is no god beside me. I put to death and I bring to life.**
>
> *Deuteronomy 32:39*

> **You shall not murder.**
>
> *Exodus 2:13*

Some Jews use these statements by God in the Torah to claim that abortion is never lawful.

Most rabbis claim that life does not begin until the foetus is able to exist on its own outside the uterus. This is based on Exodus 21:22–23: 'If men who are fighting hit a pregnant woman and she gives birth prematurely but there is no serious injury, the offender must be fined whatever the woman's husband demands and the court allows. But if there is serious injury, you are to take life for life.'

Many rabbis add to the Jewish teaching that you can kill in self-defence, and say that abortion is allowed if the pregnancy threatens the life of the mother.

Other rabbis argue that as life does not begin until birth, and as Jews are to prevent avoidable suffering, abortion is allowable if there is a risk that the baby will be seriously deformed.

FACTFILE 43

HINDUISM AND ABORTION

> **Unborn, eternal, everlasting he (the soul) primeval: he is not slain when the body is slain. If a man knows him as indestructible, eternal, unborn, never to pass away, how and whom can he cause to be slain or slay?**
>
> *Gita 2:20-21*

There are many different views on abortion among Hindus.

Some are totally opposed to abortion in any form:

> Do not have an abortion and do not keep the company of such women who have. Do not keep the company of a woman who encourages or assists in abortion.

Shikshapatri of Lord Swaminarayan.

Others use the teachings of leaders like Gandhi on ahimsa (that violence should only be used as a last resort and avoided wherever possible) to claim that abortion is only allowable if the mother's life is threatened.

Abortion is available on demand in India. 83 per cent of the population is Hindu and 5 million abortions a year are carried out, so it would appear that many Hindus approve of abortion. Some of those who do, base their approval on the teachings of Krishna in the Bhagavad Gita that you cannot harm the soul. If an abortion is carried out, then that soul will simply be born in another body.

All religions see babies as a sacred gift from God.

EUTHANASIA – THE ACTION OF INDUCING A QUIET AND EASY DEATH

SOCIAL FACTS ON EUTHANASIA

There are several ways in which this can be done:

SUICIDE – WHERE A PERSON KNOWS THEY HAVE A VERY PAINFUL, TERMINAL (GOING TO END IN DEATH) DISEASE AND COMMIT SUICIDE TO GIVE THEMSELVES A QUIET AND EASY DEATH.

ASSISTED SUICIDE – WHERE A PERSON HAS SUCH A PAINFUL TERMINAL DISEASE THAT THEY CANNOT OBTAIN THE MEANS FOR SUICIDE, SO THEY ASK SOMEONE TO GIVE THEM THE MEANS AND THEN THEY COMMIT SUICIDE.

VOLUNTARY EUTHANASIA – WHERE A PERSON HAS A PAINFUL, TERMINAL DISEASE AND CANNOT DO ANYTHING FOR THEMSELVES, SO THEY ASK SOMEONE ELSE TO KILL THEM PAINLESSLY E.G. BY THE DOCTOR GIVING THEM A LETHAL DOSE OF PAINKILLERS.

NON-VOLUNTARY EUTHANASIA – WHERE A PERSON IS NOT KEPT ALIVE BECAUSE THEY ARE REGARDED AS HAVING A LIFE WORSE THAN DEATH, BUT CANNOT MAKE ANY DECISIONS FOR THEMSELVES E.G. BABIES BORN WITH TERRIBLE ABNORMALITIES AND IN GREAT PAIN; PEOPLE ON LIFE-SUPPORT MACHINES WHO ARE 'BRAIN DEAD', PEOPLE IN COMAS WHO HAVE TO BE FED INTRAVENOUSLY.

NOT STRIVING TO KEEP ALIVE – THIS IS THE IDEA USED IN MEDICINE THAT IF SOMEONE IS SUFFERING FROM A TERMINAL ILLNESS, EVERYTHING POSSIBLE SHOULD BE DONE TO CURE THEM, AFTER THIS THEY SHOULD BE GIVEN PAINKILLERS. BUT IF, FOR EXAMPLE, THEY HAVE A HEART ATTACK, YOU DO NOT NEED TO GO THROUGH ALL THE RESUSCITATION PROCEDURES.

DOUBLE EFFECT – THIS IS THE SAME IDEA AS USED IN ABORTION, THAT IF YOU GIVE A PATIENT DRUGS TO RELIEVE THEIR PAIN, KNOWING THAT THEY WILL KILL THEM OVER A PERIOD OF TIME, THAT IS OK BECAUSE YOU ARE AIMING TO RELIEVE THE PAIN, NOT KILL THEM. IT IS USUALLY CLAIMED THAT THIS IS VERY DIFFERENT FROM GIVING THEM ONE DOSE OF PAINKILLERS SUFFICIENT TO KILL THEM STRAIGHT AWAY.

The law in Britain does not allow anyone to end another person's life either by giving drugs or by switching off a machine, even if the person requests it.

Under British law at the moment all these forms of euthanasia, except suicide, are crimes – though switching off life-support machines is covered by the idea of not 'striving officiously to keep alive'.

This is a very 'grey' area in British law and many doctors would argue that they have to strive to keep people alive otherwise they are killing them.

However, many people feel that the law needs to be changed. They think this because:

- Advances in medicine have led to people being kept alive who would previously have died, but their quality of life is appalling. It is claimed that doctors and relatives should be able to give such people a painless death.

- The development of life support machines has already brought in a form of euthanasia as doctors and relatives can agree to switch off these machines if the doctors feel there is no chance of the person regaining consciousness. It is claimed that the National Health Service cannot afford to keep people alive for years on a life support machine, which could also be used to save the life of someone else who has a chance of recovery.

- Doctors already make decisions about switching off life support machines, and various decisions by judges have given doctors the right to stop treatment. For example, Tony Bland a Hillsborough disaster victim, whose parents won the right to stop him being fed.

- Many people feel that a basic human right is to have control of your life. If you have the right to commit suicide, then you have the right to ask a doctor to assist your suicide if you are ill and in pain and unable to commit suicide yourself. The Voluntary Euthanasia Society provide 'Living Wills' where a person can write a will whilst they are fit and well saying that they do not want medical treatment if they develop an incurable disease (or out of their mind with something like Alzheimer's). This type of euthanasia, including being able to request a painless death, is now permissible in Holland.

A photograph taken from a home video of James Brady, who asked his family to kill him as he was suffering from Huntington's Chorea, a hereditary disease which leads to total debility.

All Christians agree that euthanasia, as such, is wrong. Life is given by God, and only God can take life. Human life is a gift from God and it is the duty of Christians to preserve life and to improve life.

It is the teaching of all the Churches that euthanasia in the form of the deliberate killing of a person is a grave sin. However, there are disagreements among Christians as to what to do about patients who are incurably ill and are only being kept alive by intrusive treatment, and patients who are in a persistent vegetative state (PVS or brain-dead).

The Roman Catholic Church teaches that Christians can never hasten death. Any action which is intended to cause death to relieve suffering (e.g. giving a dying person a drug overdose) is wrong. In the same way any omission of treatment in order to cause death is wrong (e.g. not giving insulin to a dying diabetic). Catholics and most other Christians would regard both of these as euthanasia and wrong.

Christians base these beliefs on the Christian teaching about the sanctity of life, the belief that only God has the right to take life.

CHRISTIANITY AND EUTHANASIA

> If we live, we live to the Lord; and if we die, we die to the Lord. So whether we live or die, we belong to the Lord.

Romans 14:8

Dr David Moore, a family doctor in Newcastle upon Tyne admitted helping many terminally ill patients to a pain free death.

FACTFILE 46

ISLAM AND EUTHANASIA

> **Nor can a soul die except by God's leave, the term being fixed as by writing.**
>
> *Surah 3:145*

> **O ye who believe... do not kill yourselves: for verily God hath been to you most merciful.**
>
> *Surah 4:29*

The Prophet said, 'In the time before you, a man was wounded. His wounds troubled him so much that he took a knife and cut his wrist to bleed himself to death. Thereupon Allah said, 'My slave hurried in the matter of his life therefore he is deprived of the Garden.'

Hadith reported in al'Bukhari and Muslim.

For these reasons Muslims do not allow euthanasia in any form. This life is a test and to use euthanasia is like cheating. It is up to God to decide when the test will end. As Muslims believe they must pass God's test to get to heaven, they cannot accept euthanasia. However, Muslim lawyers have recently agreed to allow the switching off of life support machines if doctors agree that life has ended.

FACTFILE 47

JUDAISM AND EUTHANASIA

The Biblical teachings which Jews use to oppose abortion are used to oppose euthanasia. Most rabbis would claim any form of euthanasia is wrong.

> If there is anything which causes a hindrance to the departure of the soul... then it is permissible to remove it.

Rabbi Moses Isserles.

Some rabbis use this statement to argue in favour of switching off life-support machines and 'not striving officiously' to keep alive. If humans are striving officiously to stop someone dying, they are interfering with God's will.

FACTFILE 48

HINDUISM AND EUTHANASIA

> Non-violence is the highest ethical code of behaviour. It includes non-killing, non-injury and non-harming. Do not kill any living creature... Do not kill a human being... Do not commit suicide.

Shikshapatri of Lord Swaminarayan.

This simple summary of the doctrine of ahimsa is used by many Hindus to ban euthanasia in any form.

Many Hindus use the teaching in the Bhagavad Gita in support of euthanasia (see page 86). It is impossible to harm the soul so easing the soul's progress to its next life – by switching off a life-support machine, or by 'not striving officiously to keep alive' – is allowed.

Factfile 34 The sanctity of life

Write down three reasons why Christians believe life is sacred.

Factfiles 35, 36, 37, 38 Christian, Muslim, Jewish and Hindu teaching on life after death

1 Have a class discussion on whether there is life after death. Then write down the main arguments for and against.

2 Make a chart to show the main differences between resurrection of the body and immortality of the soul. Indicate on the chart which one Christians believe in and what the members of one other religion believe about life after death.

3 'Once you're dead, you're dead. There can be no life after death.' Do you agree? Give reasons for your opinion, showing you have considered another point of view.

Factfile 39 Social facts on abortion

Have a class discussion on why abortion was legalised in Britain and whether the law now needs to be changed.

Factfile 40 Christianity and abortion

'No Christian should ever have an abortion.' Do you agree? Give reasons for your answer, showing that you have considered another point of view.

Factfiles 41, 42, 43 Islam, Judaism, Hinduism and abortion

Choose one of these religions. Write down whether they allow or disallow abortion and two of their reasons for this attitude.

Factfile 44 Social facts on euthanasia

1 Write down the differences between suicide, voluntary euthanasia and involuntary euthanasia.

2 Discuss in a group why euthanasia has become more of an issue in the last 20 years.

Factfiles 45, 46, 47, 48 Christian, Islamic, Jewish and Hindu attitudes to euthanasia

1 Write down two Christian arguments and two arguments from one other religion against euthanasia.

2 'If I were on a life-support machine and brain dead, I would want my relatives or friends to switch it off.'
Do you agree? Give your reasons for your opinion, showing that you have considered another point of view.

RELIGION AND THE MEDIA

FACTFILE 49

INTRODUCTION

When television began, religious broadcasts were aimed at an audience which went to church fairly regularly and which accepted all traditional Christian beliefs. At that time there were very few Hindus, Muslims and Sikhs in the United Kingdom, and the main non-Christian faith was Judaism. So all religious broadcasting has its roots in the Christian Churches.

However, as religious broadcasting has changed, so has its target audience. David Kremer, the new programmes editor for BBC Religious Broadcasting, regards his target audience as the 'vaguely religious'. By this he means those people who believe in God and in life having a purpose, but only go to church for such things as baptisms, weddings and funerals (rites of passage).

There are still a few programmes which remain aimed at the religiously committed audience such as the worship programmes in Advent, the meditation programmes at Easter and the various programmes for special religious festivals in the ethnic minority religions (Ramadan, Jewish New Year, Diwali all have special programmes on late at night).

Religious broadcasters accept that they cannot devote a great deal of time to the faiths of the ethnic minorities, although they would like to do so. However, they have to look at the potential audience. BBC1 is a popular channel which needs to attract at least 20 per cent of those watching television at any time and the ethnic minorities only account for 5 per cent of the population. Nevertheless as religious broadcasting becomes more and more aimed at the 'vaguely religious' rather than committed Christians, it is likely that more time will be devoted to non-Christian religions if it is thought the 'vaguely religious' may be interested in them.

These changes have caused problems with the leadership of the Churches. The Archbishop of York wrote to the Government in December 1998 to complain about 'the marginalisation of religion' by the BBC. He was particularly concerned that there would be no broadcast of a church service on Christmas Day 1998. Instead BBC1 had a morning programme of popular carols and Christmas music, and an evening programme *The People's Nativity* with celebrities reading from the Christmas story. The Archbishop of York is the chairman of the Central Religious Advisory Council (CRAC) a multi-faith body which advises the BBC and ITV on religious broadcasting.

> - Where have we come from?
> - Why are we here?
> - How should we live?
>
> 'BBC Religion exists to ask the big questions that underlie all human life and explore the different ways in which people try to answer them, whether through worship, prayer, or simply giving food for thought

The aim of Religious Broadcasting by the BBC.

Pam Rhodes presents the most popular religious broadcast, *Songs of Praise*.

At a time when religious broadcasting is being increasingly marginalised, particularly with the abolition of ITV's God Slot, Channel 4 is renewing its commitment to religious broadcasting by launching *Witness*, a prestigious new strand of documentaries about personal belief and scheduling them in peak time at 9.00 p.m. There has never been a major strand like this in peak-time before – the BBC's Sunday religious documentary strands are much later at night.

Although more British people watch religious TV programmes than attend football matches, there is still a large proportion of viewers who are reluctant to watch programmes of an overtly religious nature. Personal beliefs, however, affect our lives and the decisions we make on an everyday basis... What previously seemed exclusively religious preoccupations – abortion or euthanasia, for instance – have come to the forefront of contemporary argument.

Religious broadcasting may be in retreat on other channels, but not on Channel 4. *Witness* is our latest initiative and it attempts to do for religion what *Cutting Edge* does for our documentaries.

Michael Grade Chief Executive Channel 4.

WORSHIP AND MAGAZINE PROGRAMMES

The Heaven and Earth Show is religious daytime TV.

Both ITV and BBC now also produce meditation type programmes (usually fairly late on weeknights rather than on Sundays) whenever there is a religious festival for Islam, Judaism, Hinduism or Sikhism. These programmes tend to focus on members of the faith living in Britain and what the festival means for them.

There is a wide range of worship and magazine programmes shown on terrestrial television. Some appear every Sunday, others at various times around the year.

The most popular specifically religious programme is *Songs of Praise*. This programme attracts audiences of between five and seven million every Sunday in the God-slot time around 6.00 p.m.

When it first began, *Songs of Praise* was simply hymn singing in a church with a prayer or two. However, the programme has changed as television audiences have changed. Hugh Faupel, editor of *Songs of Praise*, says that, 'Songs of Praise is now an inspirational programme aimed at touching people's lives'.

The programme now has much more than hymn singing. There is usually some form of inspirational music performance. In 1998 these were provided by such people as Lesley Garrett, 911 and Jimmy Ruffin. There are also human interest stories from ordinary people and how faith has touched their lives. These are similar to interviews in chat shows, but much more related to religious faith.

ITV still has a Sunday morning God-slot when it usually broadcasts an entire Christian service live from a church. This provides worship for those unable to get to church and may be watched by the 'vaguely religious' audience.

BBC1 has recently replaced its Christian worship type programmes on Sunday morning by the more daytime television programme *The Heaven and Earth Show*. This is presented by Simon Biagi and Amanda Redington sitting on a sofa and there is a phone-in for every item so that the audience can be involved.

The programme lasts for a whole hour and typical programme had the following items:

- The Mind and Body Festival in Manchester with discussion of New Age ideas and alternative medicine;
- an interview with Yuri Geller discussing his alleged psychic powers, from fork bending to mind-reading Russian politicians for the CIA;
- recipes for Sunday lunch;
- sex, lies and cover up – a discussion with two American Christians about whether President Clinton should carry on as President and whether leaders should be sexually moral;
- a documentary about the problems of transporting the 300-strong Mormon Tabernacle choir to appear on *Songs of Praise* at the Albert Hall;
- a discussion on the B-Sky-B take-over of Manchester United related to the morality of extreme wealth;
- a mini-documentary on a police detective who is a medium at Wimbledon Christian Spiritualist Church followed by phone-in discussion;
- a reading of inspiritional poetry.

ITV now shows its magazine type programmes late on Sunday evening either *Sunday Night* or *Holy Smoke* (a religious programme aimed specifically at under 25's) are broadcast around midnight.

Channel 5 usually has religious programmes on between 8.00 a.m. and 9.00 a.m. on a Sunday morning. These include *Alpha Zone*, about the religious music scene, and *My Sunday* which focuses on the faith of 'people in the public eye'.

Apart from *Songs of Praise*, religious documentaries are the most popular religious broadcasts. This is perhaps because they are little different in format from any other documentary. They also deal with issues which are of interest to most people, not just the very religious.

BBC1 has a religious documentary every Sunday evening between 10.30 and 11.30 – either *Everyman* or *Heart of the Matter*. *Everyman* tends to be more of a documentary using mainly film, whereas *Heart of the Matter* begins with a short documentary and then tends to have a studio discussion on the issues raised. These programmes usually attract an audience of around two million.

The 1998–99 programmes dealt with a wide range of issues: transplant surgery; baby L in New Zealand whose parents wanted her to live, but the doctors took action to let her die because she was so handicapped; the CIA in Tibet using Buddhism; whether it is possible to contact the dead; child berearvment; surviving Lockerbie; couples married to a partner of a different religion; an investigation into whether there has already been a woman Pope.

The main ITV religious documentary at the moment is Channel 4's *Witness* broadcast on Thursday evenings at 9.00 p.m. It is also aimed at a more general audience investigating issues which affect 'the individual's search for truth.' *Witness* has investigated issues such as black churches in South Africa; the variety and weirdness of religion in Los Angeles; and modern Nazis who deny that the Holocaust ever took place.

RELIGIOUS DOCUMENTARIES

One *Everyman* programme was about British Muslim converts.

As well as these, both BBC2 and ITV also commission one-off religious documentaries. BBC2 has been responsible for two great series on religion: *The Long Search* which looked at the six main world religions in humanity's search for God and *The Sea of Faith* which looked at the impact of science and philosophy on religion since the time of Galileo. They have also done series on Islam, *The Living World of Islam* and people's attitudes to holy books, *Going by the Book*.

Channel 4 produced *Testament* about the origins and development of the Bible and ITV has had Tuesday documentaries about Mother Theresa and other figures working for the poor because of their religious beliefs.

RELIGIOUS AND MORAL ISSUES IN SOAPS AND DRAMA

You are required to study a religious or moral issue in a soap opera or the national daily press. To do this, it is important to choose an issue and say why it is an issue.

A **religious issue** is an issue connected with the meaning of life, or with some particular religious practice about which people argue for example, is there life after death? Does God exist? Should religious cults have the freedom to convert anyone? Should priests be able to marry? Should women be able to be priests? Should Muslim girls be free to marry Christian boys?

A **moral issue** is an argument about whether some type of action is right or wrong (often moral issues are religious issues as well because all religions have their own moral principles and teachings) for example, is it right to get divorced when young children are involved? Is it right to have an abortion if your child will be handicapped? Should people suffering in great pain from a terminal disease be allowed to have an assisted suicide or euthanasia?

Here are a few such issues from soap operas to show you how these programmes can illustrate religious and moral issues.

Eastenders featured a religious issue when the vicar, Alex, was attracted to Kathy Beale and began an affair with her. The programme explored the issue of how a vicar can become too closely involved when helping women with problems (Kathy's husband had become an alcoholic) and Alex's dilemma of whether to follow his love for Kathy or his love for God.

Coronation Street featured a religious issue when Zoe's baby died of meningitis and she blamed herself. In her despair she joined a religious cult which promised her that she would be with her baby again in the after life. The programme explored the issue of religious cults and the way in which religion can break up a relationship if only one of the partners believes (Zoe's partner, Ashley, felt the cult was dangerous and wanted to get Zoe away from it). It also touched, occasionally, on the issue of life after death.

Eastenders featured a moral issue when Ian and Cindy Beale's marriage broke up and they fought over the custody of the children, involving kidnappings, flight to Italy and shootings by hired killers. All of this explored the issues of adultery, divorce and the way in which children can be used as pawns in battles between parents in the name of love.

Brookside investigates many religious and moral issues, including the incestuous relationship between a brother and sister, a son-in-law being put on trial for mercy-killing and a surrogate mother. *Brookside* certainly feels that religious and moral issues bring life and viewers to a soap.

You also have to study a religious theme or themes in a film or television drama.

The film *Priest* has a clearly religious theme. It is all about a young Roman Catholic priest and the problems he faces in trying to be a priest in the 1990's. The main theme is whether Roman Catholic priests should be celibate and whether homosexual sex is an unforgivable sin for a priest. However, the film also deals with the relationship between the Old and New Testaments and whether human beings have free will.

Other films which have religious themes are: *Four Weddings and a Funeral* (issues include: the purpose of marriage: should people use churches just as places for weddings and funerals; the purpose of life); *Contact* whose religious theme is whether or not God exists; *Star Wars* whose religious theme is whether there is a force for good in the universe (God) which will not let evil triumph.

Many television dramas have religious themes. One of the clearest of these was *Ballykissangel* in which a young English Roman Catholic priest fell in love with an Irish atheist and had to resist his emotions to keep his priesthood.

You must be very clear what the religious theme is in any film or drama you choose, why this theme is important and was chosen by the director and how the theme is developed.

Dervla Kirwin and Stephen Tompkinson in Ballykissangel explored the issue of Catholic priests falling in love.

QUESTIONS

1 What is the 'God-slot'?

2 Which programme is still in the 'God-slot'?

3 Give two reasons why Channel 4 decided to put a religious programme on at peak viewing time.

Factfile 50 Worship and magazine programmes

Watch *Songs of Praise, The Heaven and Earth Show* and one other worship or magazine programme. During and after viewing the programme, answer these questions:
(a) What is the target audience?
(b) Why might people in that target audience enjoy it?
(c) Why might other viewers not enjoy it?

Factfile 51 Religious documentaries

1 Watch at least two religious documentary-type programmes. During and after viewing write down answers to the following:
   (a) Who might watch a programme like this?
   (b) Why would they find it interesting?
   (c) Why might some viewers find it uninteresting?

2 Have a class discussion on why television produces a wide range of religious programmes.

Factfile 52 Religious and moral issues in soaps and dramas

1 Use the Radio/TV Times to find a soap which is dealing with a religious or moral issue. Watch the soap regularly and write down:
   (a) what the issue is;
   (b) who is involved;
   (c) how the issue ends.

2 Then answer the following questions:
   (a) Why did the soap deal with this issue?
   (b) In what other ways could the issue have been dealt with?
   (c) Which ways would you have dealt with the issue and why?

3 Watch a film or television drama with a religious theme. Write down:
   (a) what the theme was;
   (b) how it was dealt with;
   (c) why you think it was chosen;
   (d) how effective you thought it was and why.

RELIGION, WEALTH AND POVERTY

Christians believe that wealth is something which can be used for good or evil, and so, in itself, is not a bad thing. Christians can only gain money in lawful and moral ways and when they have wealth, it is a gift from God not theirs alone. Many biblical teachings show that if you have the wrong attitude to money, wealth can lead you away from God:

Jesus told a parable about the end of the world when everyone would come before him to be judged. The good and bad would be separated like sheep and goats are separated by a shepherd. The good would be sent to heaven because, as Jesus said, 'When I was hungry you fed me. When I was thirsty, you gave me drink, when I was naked you clothed me. When I was sick or in prison you visited me.' The good people wanted to know when they had ever done this and Jesus said, 'When you did it for the least of my brothers, you did it for me.' The bad people were told they were going to hell because they had never fed the hungry, given drink to the thirsty, clothed the naked or visited those who were sick or in prison. When they asked when they had never done these things, Jesus said, 'When you did not do it for other people, you did not do it for me.'
(based on Matthew 25:31–46)

In the parable of the Good Samaritan Jesus showed that the commandment to Christians to love God and love their neighbour means they must help anyone who is in trouble whether they live next door or far away (Luke 10:25–37).

So Christians believe they must share their wealth with the poor:

> God blesses those who come to the aid of the poor and rebukes those who turn away from them... Love for the poor is incompatible with immoderate use of riches or their selfish use.

Catechism of the Catholic Church.

> The Church should concern itself first, and indeed second, with the poor and needy, whether in spirit or in body.

A statement by the Archbishops' Commission on Church and State quoted in *Faith in the City* a Church of England report on poverty and the Church in Great Britain.

FACTFILE 53

CHRISTIAN TEACHING ON WEALTH AND POVERTY

People who want to get rich fall into temptation and a trap and into many foolish and harmful desires that plunge men into ruin and destruction. For the love of money is a root of all kinds of evil.

1 Timothy 6:9-10

Jesus looked at him and loved him. 'One thing you lack,' he said. 'Go sell everything you have and give to the poor, and you will have treasure in heaven. Then come, follow me.' At this the man's face fell. He went away sad because he had great wealth. Jesus looked round and said to his disciples, 'How hard it is for the rich to enter the kingdom of God.'

Mark 10:21-23

'No one can serve two masters. Either he will hate the one and love the other, or he will be devoted to the one and despise the other. You cannot serve both God and Money.'

Matthew 6:24

According to the *New Testament* our riches must be used for the help of others, especially the poor. Christians believe that all humans are equal in the eyes of God and that all the good things of the earth have been given to us by God to use to help each other:

> **If anyone has material possessions and sees his brother in need, how can the love of God be in him? Dear children let us not love with words or tongue, but with actions and in truth.**

1 John 3:17,18

> **What good is it, my brothers, if a man claims to have faith but has no deeds? Can his faith save him? Suppose a brother or sister is without clothes and daily food. If one of you says to him, 'Go I wish you well; keep warm and well-fed,' but does nothing about his physical needs, what good is it? In the same way faith by itself, if it is not accompanied by action is dead.**

James 2:14–17

This means that Christians are not just concerned about the poor in Great Britain:

> Rich nations have a grave moral responsibility towards those which are unable to ensure the means of their development by themselves.

Catechism of the Catholic Church.

> Particularly since the second world war, countless resolutions and reports have been adopted by the Methodist Conference recognising the obligation laid upon Christians to go to the relief of those in need, to ensure rehabilitation after natural or man-made disasters, and to assist in fundamental development – so as to enable people to become responsible for their own futures.

Methodist statement in What the Churches say on Moral Issues.

> Following a United Nations recommendation that the developed nations should spend 1% of their Gross National Product on overseas aid, the Presbyterian and Congregational Churches in England and Wales, before their union as the URC in 1972, established a World Development 1% Appeal to match the call to governments. The appeal was for 1% of annual take-home pay...This self-tax was a sign of commitment to the human family and of Christian hope which refuses to be paralysed in the face of human suffering and deprivation.

Statement by the URC in What the Churches say on Moral Issues.

What overpopulation? Africa can grow enough to feed its people and Europe pays farmers not to farm.

Islam teaches that wealth is something given by God for the benefit of humanity and, therefore, is something to be shared. In Islam, sharing your wealth is not an optional extra, it is something commanded by God in the religious pillar of *Zakah*. In Arabic, Zakah means purification and many Muslims believe that giving Zakah purifies the money you have left so that no harm can come to you from it. There is a hadith which says, 'Protect your property by giving Zakah and help your relatives to recover from disease by giving charity.'

Muslims pay Zakah annually on the basis of two and a half percent of all their savings and income above the level needed to keep their family. They also pay a special zakah to the poor on their festival of Id ul'Fit'r.

Muslims also believe in paying Sadaqah, voluntary giving to charity if ever they are asked, or if they have any spare cash.

Muslims are also encouraged to help the poor by giving interest-free loans (the acceptance or payment or interest is banned in Islam). If the poor find it difficult to repay, Muslims are encouraged to change the loan to a gift.

For these reasons Muslims help the poor in Great Britain through the Zakah of the mosque which provides funds for poor Muslim families. Others send their charity to help the poor in impoverished countries. Often a mosque in Pakistan, Bangladesh or Gujarat will send to a British mosque asking for money to help with things like wells and medical work. There are also Muslim charities such as Muslim Aid and Islamic Relief which provide help for people in Less Developed Countries.

MUSLIM TEACHING ON WEALTH AND POVERTY

> Those who in charity spend of their goods by night and by day, in secret and in public, have their reward with their Lord.

Surah 2:274

> If the debtor is in a difficulty, grant him time to repay. But if ye remit it by way of charity, that is best for you if ye only knew.

Surah 2:280

> He who eats and drinks whilst his brother goes hungry is not one of us.

Hadith quoted by al'Bukhari.

Muslim Aid helped construct the school building of an orphanage in Bulamagi, Uganda.

JEWISH TEACHING ON WEALTH AND POVERTY

The Torah shows how wealth is to be used to help the poor:

> When you reap the harvest of your land, do not reap to the very edge of your field or gather the gleanings of your harvest. Do not go over your vineyard a second time or pick up the grapes that have fallen. Leave them for the poor and the alien.

Leviticus 19:9–10

> If there is a poor man among your brothers in any of the towns of the land that the Lord your God is giving you, do not be hard-hearted or tight-fisted towards your brother. Rather be open-handed and freely lend him whatever he needs.

Deuteronomy 15:7–8

> Hear this you who trample the needy and do away with the poor of the land, saying, 'When will the New Moon be over that we may sell grain, and the sabbath be ended that we may market wheat?' – skimping the measure, boosting the price and cheating with dishonest scales, buying the poor with silver and the needy for a pair of sandals, selling even the sweepings of the wheat. The Lord has sworn by the Pride of Jacob, 'I will never forget anything they have done.'

Amos 8:4–7

Judaism teaches that wealth is a gift from God and is to be used both for yourself and for others. The Tenakh makes quite clear that a Jew can only make money in the correct way (one which keeps the mitzvot).

Jews are expected to give one tenth of their income to the poor as *tzedakah* (often translated as charity, but really meaning correctness – by giving to the poor you are using money correctly and putting the poor back into their correct position). Many Jews follow the teachings of Maimonides on giving charity – the best form of charity makes sure that the poor will never need charity again.

The Talmud states that Rabbi Eleazar used to give a coin to a poor man and then say his prayers because it is written, 'I in righteousness shall behold thy face' (Psalm 17:15). This means, when I am in righteousness by giving charity (tzedakah) then I shall behold thy face, appear before you in prayer. This is the basis for the custom of the charity box in the synagogue. During the week, before the service begins, everyone has the opportunity of training himself to live and let live by dropping in some coins for charity.

At home, every member of a Jewish family is given a similar training through a charity box. At times of celebration or good fortune, it is usual to put money in the box in gratitude to God.

There are many Jewish charities operating in Great Britain, especially Jewish Care. Jews also help the poor in less developed countries.

World Jewish Relief sends aid from British Jews to relieve disasters worldwide. Here medical and food aid arrives for all the people of Bosnia.

Hindus believe that wealth is a good thing if it has been gained by lawful means. If you follow your *dharma* (social duty) in your *ashrama* (stage of life) and this allows you to gain wealth in a lawful way, then you should enjoy the wealth.

This teaching was also emphasised by Kautilya who wrote the *Artha-shastra* in about 300 BCE. Artha is Sanskrit for wealth and this book is all about how to gain and use wealth and power morally and religiously.

So, many Hindus are involved in projects to provide education, healthcare, food and jobs for the poor of India. All Hindu temples collect charity gifts which are used either to help poor Hindus in Great Britain or to help projects in India.

Many British Hindus are in direct contact with Hindus in India who are working on projects to help the poor and send money directly to them. Most of the schemes established in India to help the poor have been set up by Hindus or by the Government which is mainly Hindu. For example, the Swaminarayan Hindu Mission in the UK (known worldwide as Bochasanwasi Shri Akshar Purashottam Swaminarayan Sanstha – BAPS) is actively involved through a network of volunteers in relief work especially in India. BAPS had a large contribution in rehabilitating victims of the earthquake in Latur and are also currently involved in rebuilding ten schools within the cyclone affected region of Kandla.

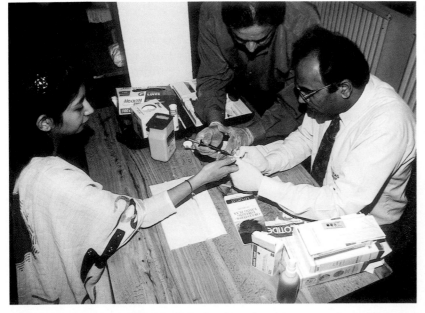

The Swaminarayan Hindu Mission's volunteers carrying out health checks.

HINDU TEACHING ON WEALTH AND POVERTY

Whether he is well-off or in distress, he must not pursue wealth through degrading or harmful activities, nor through forbidden occupations, nor through accepting presents from others.

Law of Manu 4:18

Do not gamble, do not steal; not even for a religious or benevolent cause... do not accept bribes.

Maintain a daily account of income and expenditure. Do not indulge in extravagant expenses... Do not keep the clearance of a debt a secret affair.

Pay the correct wages... to the workers employed by you... take good care of your servants.

Be kind and charitable towards the deserving ones.

Serve fellow beings in their illness and distress.

Spread of knowledge and education is a great meritorious deed. If possible either aid or establish an educational institution... to spread the right knowledge on earth.

Shikshapatri of Lord Swaminarayan.

THE NEED FOR WORLD DEVELOPMENT

From about 1950 to 1985, it was common to talk of poor countries as 'Third World' countries. This was because some thinkers divided the world into three:

• First World – the West (USA, Western Europe, Canada, Australia, New Zealand, Japan).

• Second World – the communist countries (USSR, Eastern Europe, China). These were regarded as poorer than the West, but richer than the rest of the world.

• Third World – all the other countries, which were regarded as the poorest countries of the world.

Many books may still refer to 'Third World' countries.

More recently it has been seen that world poverty is a very complex issue. Some countries once regarded as Third World are now richer than the West (e.g. Brunei, Kuwait, Singapore). Others are not as rich as the West, but are not poverty stricken. So now the countries of the world may again be divided into three groups, but in a very different way:

• developed countries – rich countries like USA and Western Europe;

• developing countries – countries which are becoming richer like Brazil, Mexico, Malaysia;

• less developed countries (LDC's) – countries which are still very poor and have people starving like Sudan, Bangladesh, Mali.

Reasons for lack of development

Wars

Wars destroy crops, homes, schools, hospitals etc. causing even more poverty. They also force many people to leave their homes and become refugees in other safer countries. These neighbouring countries may have been developing, but a sudden influx of refugees with no money or food can make that country poor again.

Many LDC's have been badly affected by wars. In Africa, many civil wars (wars fought between people from the same country) have been caused by European empire-building in the nineteenth century. Several African races were joined into one country even though half a race was in another country. When these countries achieved independence, they were still artificial countries and one race was often badly treated by the ruling race resulting in civil war (as has happened in Europe since the various parts of Yugoslavia were given independence). LDC's can also suffer from wars between countries e.g. Ethiopia and Somalia, Afghanistan and Russia; and from wars caused by corruption and political differences e.g. Mozambique, Angola, Guatemala.

Natural Disasters

Many LDC's are situated in areas of the world where natural disasters (earthquakes, floods, droughts etc.) are more frequent and more severe than anywhere else. An earthquake or a flood, for example, can destroy many thousands of homes and the farmland on which the inhabitants depend. If rain does not fall, crops will not grow unless you have the wealth to sink wells, install pumps and organise an irrigation system.

Debt

Most LDC's have to borrow money from the banks of developed countries to survive and begin to develop. However, these banks charge interest, so that a less developed country can find itself paying more in interest than they earn in foreign currency. In the early seventies, for example, Chile borrowed 3.9 billion dollars. By 1982, she had paid 12.8 billion dollars in interest, but still owed money.

This extra 9 billion dollars could have been used to speed up Chile's development, instead it went to countries that are already rich.

Cash Crops

The only way many LDC's can make enough money for their debts is to grow cash crops (crops grown for sale rather than consumption). Cotton, coffee, tea and tobacco are grown to sell to the developed world. Many people in LDC's are starving because land is used to grow cash crops instead of food.

There are other factors contributing to world poverty: lack of education, lack of clean fresh water, disease, low life expectancy leading to large numbers of children, relying on one export (e.g. copper or oil) whose value may go down in the world market changing a country from rich to poor almost overnight.

> World poverty concerns us all because we are all dependent on each other – if we want the Sudanese to grow cotton for our clothes, we must be prepared to make sure that the Sudanese have enough food.

'Give a man a fish; feed him for a day. Teach a man to fish; feed him for a lifetime.' Gipsies cleaning fishing nets in Goa, India.

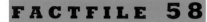
THE WORK OF CHRISTIAN ORGANISATIONS TO RELIEVE POVERTY

The Salvation Army was founded by William Booth in 1865. He was concerned about the poor of the inner-cities and that the churches were doing nothing for them. The Salvation Army believed that the poor working class needed to be brought into the church by evangelisation (preaching about Jesus) in the streets and pubs and using the sort of music heard in music halls (the nineteenth-century equivalent of night clubs).

However, it also believed that the poor needed to be shown the love of Jesus in practical ways. So the early Salvation Army ran soup kitchens, hostels for the homeless and for unmarried mothers who were often thrown onto the streets by their disgusted parents.

Hungry and homeless, as in the parable of the Sheep and the Goats.

Today, the Salvation Army tries to help the poor in Britain in the following ways:

1 It runs hostels in city centres for homeless men and goes out at night on 'soup runs' taking hot food to those who are sleeping rough.

2 It provides facilities for the poor, as most Salvation Army citadels (churches) are in the inner-city or town centre. It runs lunch clubs for the over-sixties and provides a variety of children's and young people's clubs.

3 It runs rehabilitation centres for alcoholics and drug addicts. The Salvation Army believed from its beginning that alcohol and drugs make people poor and have disastrous effects on family life. All Salvationists have to sign a statement when they become a member promising to avoid alcohol, tobacco and drugs. The Salvation Army tries to prevent addiction by visiting pubs and places where drugs are used and by selling the *War Cry* magazine.

Although all their work is done in the name of Jesus, the Salvation Army gives help and care to the poor without asking about their attitude to religion.

The Salvation Army finances its work for the poor by raising money through flag days and playing carols etc. with their brass bands. They also receive grants from the government and local authority social services for their hostels.

Christian Aid and poverty overseas

Christian Aid began as the British Churches Ecumenical Refugee Council set up in 1944 to help the hundreds of thousands of Europeans who had been made homeless by the Second World War. In September 1945, it became Christian Aid, a department of the British Council of Churches (all the non-Roman Catholic Churches) providing help for poor people in less developed countries:

> Christian Aid works in over sixty countries providing emergency aid and long term assistance to Church and community organisations working to overcome poverty. Christian Aid prefers to work through local organisations, believing local people know best how to solve their own problems. Christian Aid works on the basis of need regardless of race or religion.

Statement of aims published by *Christian Aid News* October 1995.

Christian Aid working with villagers in Eritrea to build an earth dam.

To achieve this aim the work of Christian Aid can be split into four parts:

1 Fund-raising

In order to do any work to relieve poverty, Christian Aid needs money which is raised in several ways.

- Since 1957, Christian Aid Week has been organised as a nationwide event in May each year. Churches divide up towns between them and try to put an envelope and information sheet about the work of Christian Aid into every house. In 1995, Christian Aid Week raised £8.6 million.

- Many churches and individuals also have fund-raising events throughout the year which raise about three times as much as Christian Aid Week.

2 Emergency aid

- Christian Aid has a disaster fund to deal with natural disasters and refugees. This often has to take priority over long-term aid because without it people would die.

- The sort of help Christian Aid gives includes sending food, antibiotics and shelters to the victims in Honduras of the 1998 hurricanes, sending food to drought-stricken Zimbabwe, and sending blankets, tents and food to war refugees in Bosnia and Rwanda.

- Christian Aid spends between 10 per cent and 15 per cent of its funds each year on emergency aid.

3 Long-term aid

- Christian Aid has an advantage over many charities because it is in contact with organisations at the receiving end of aid. Much of Christian Aid's emergency and long-term aid is channelled through Christian organisations in the country concerned. Often these local groups come up with ideas for long-term aid which they ask Christian Aid to finance.

- In Columbia, South America, developers were threatening to drive poor farmers and their families out of their homes and also damage the environment. The farmers established an organisation and worked out a method of developing the area using alternative environmentally friendly methods which would keep their family homes. Christian Aid is working with the European Union to finance this scheme.

- In Bangladesh, Christian Aid is funding a group of Christian healthworkers who have built a factory to make basic drugs which Bangladesh cannot afford to import.

- In Lesotho, Christian Aid is financing a local Christian agricultural school which is trying to increase food production by reducing soil erosion and bringing in new, but cheap and practical, farming methods.

- In all these areas, Christian Aid sees its function as helping people to help themselves so that they will not need aid. Often this is done through the use of 'appropriate technology' (technology that can be operated and repaired by the people using it rather than needing support from outside).

4 Education

- About five per cent of Christian Aid's budget is spent on educating the people and Churches of Britain about the need for development and the way in which Christians can help less developed countries.

- It publishes a quarterly newspaper, *Christian Aid News*, and many educational materials. These not only give information about what Christian Aid is doing, but also give information about world development. What the world spends on arms in two weeks, for example, would give everyone in the world enough food, water, education and shelter for a year.

- Christian Aid also supports campaigns to improve the situation in less developed countries. For example:

Putting you in the picture

Christian Aid supports several multi-ethnic football projects in Burundi through the National Council of Churches in Burundi (CNEB). Young people have been the worst affected by Burundi's inter-ethnic conflict. Thousands of children have been orphaned and thousands more have become victims of violence – many saw their parents massacred.

Christian Aid ambassador for peace, Charton Athletic mid-fielder John Barnes.

Melchior Ndadye, Burundi's first Hutu president, was killed in a military coup in October 1993. Thousands of Tutsis were in turn murdered in the countryside by Hutu neighbours led by Hutu officials; thousands of Hutu farmers were murdered as the army re-imposed a fragile condition of order in the countryside. Today peace and reconciliation is the crucial work of groups throughout the country as communities of Hutus and Tutsis gradually begin to live together again.

Football, for Burundians from Hutu and Tutsi backgrounds, is helping to heal the scars caused by years of armed conflict. John Barnes established the John Barnes Cup to be awarded to the team which wins the league for mixed Hutu-Tutsi youth teams and to the player who does the most to promote peace in the country. 'I am delighted that sport is used in such a constructive way,' said John. 'It's essential that we try to bring young people from different ethnic groups together. After their horrific experiences of the war, I hope my being there and football can go some way towards healing the wounds.'

From the Christian Aid news release *Peace ambassador John Barnes flies back from Burundi.*

QUESTIONS

Factfile 53 Christian teaching on wealth and poverty

1 What do Christians believe is the right attitude to wealth? Give two biblical and two Church reasons for your answer.

2 Which parables did Jesus tell which encourage us to share our wealth?

3 'The love of money is the root of all evil.' Do you agree? Give reasons for your opinion, showing you have considered another point of view.

Factfiles 54, 55, 56 Muslim, Jewish and Hindu teaching on wealth and poverty

Choose one religion and write down:
(a) what it teaches about the use of wealth
(b) two reasons for those teachings.

Factfile 57 The need for world development

1 Why do some books refer to poor countries as 'Third World'?

2 Why is it more correct to use the term 'Less Developed Countries'?

3 Make a list of reasons for lack of development.

4 Use an atlas to identify an LDC in Asia, Africa and South/Central America. Check your answer with a teacher.

Factfile 58 The work of Christian organisations to relieve poverty

1 Make a list of the ways in which the Salvation Army helps poor people.

2 Give four reasons why they might do this work.

3 Why was Christian Aid set up?

4 Make a list of the ways in which Christian Aid helps Less Developed Countries.

5 Give four reasons why they do this work.

6 'Only religion can solve the problem of world poverty.' Do you agree? Give reasons for your opinion, showing you have considered another point of view.

RELIGION AND THE ENVIRONMENT

The dangers of pollution

Scientists often speak of the earth as an ecosystem. By this they mean that the plants, animals and atmosphere of the earth interact with each other to produce all the materials which are needed for life on earth to continue. The problem with an ecosystem is that it is very finely balanced and so altering one of the components can have great effects on the rest of the system (you may have heard of the chaos theory where the fluttering of an extra butterfly in Brazil results in a hurricane in Florida). The changes humans have made to the earth's ecosystem (environment) may cause similar problems. The main problems of pollution are:

- **The Greenhouse Effect**
  The burning of fossil fuels (gas, coal and oil) produces carbon dioxide. This produces a barrier in the atmosphere rather like the glass in a greenhouse so that the heat from the sun can get through, but cannot get back out again. Many scientists believe that this is causing the earth to warm up.

  A report published by the UK Climate Impacts Programme in October 1998 predicts that the amount of carbon dioxide in the atmosphere will increase by 50 per cent by 2050. This would lead to average temperatures in the south east of England rising by 1.3 degrees Celsius by 2020 and by 2 degrees Celsius by 2050. There would be a rainfall increase of 15–20 per cent in the north of England and Scotland by 2050. Other scientists have claimed that such rises in temperature will lead to a rise in the level of the sea (because of the ice-caps melting) which means some coastal areas could disappear.

- **Eutrophication**
  An excess of nitrates, nitrites and phosphates in rivers is leading to a lack of oxygen and an increase in aquatic plants which is causing fish to die and poisons to enter water supplies. This is caused by: fertilisers being washed into streams; sewage pollution and a lack of trees to soak up the nitrogen. This could lead to major health problems for humans.

- **Deforestation**
  Many scientists are also worried about the way the number of trees on earth are declining. Trees are essential for three things: in the process of photosynthesis they remove carbon dioxide from the atmosphere and put back oxygen; in the

nitrogen cycle, they soak up nitrates etc. from the soil; and they prevent soil erosion and desertification (fertile land becoming a desert). They fear that if humans go on cutting down trees (almost half the Amazonian Jungle has now been destroyed), major problems will be caused for the environment.

- **Radioactive pollution**
  Nuclear power stations do not produce carbon dioxide, but do produce nuclear waste which will take thousands if not millions of years to be safe. This waste is being buried and no one knows whether the containers it is buried in will be able to contain it safely for this length of time. When humans come into contact with too much radiation they can be killed, get cancer and have genetically mutated children as seen in the Chernobyl nuclear power station disaster of 1986.

The nuclear power station in Hartlepool.

The problem of resources

Modern society has a lifestyle which depends on finite resources (things like oil of which there is only a certain amount on the earth so that when it is used up there will be none left). One of the major finite resources is oil. It is not only petrol and diesel fuel that come from oil, all plastics come from oil as do many chemical feedstocks for animals, all road surfaces, most candles and polishes. Steel is made from iron ore, one of the many minerals which are finite resources.

Many scientists feel that unless we stop the way we are using these resources, they will soon run out. This would mean no cars, no televisions, hi-fi's etc. In other words the problem of resources could have as severe consequences as the problem of pollution.

The proper use of resources

Many scientists believe that science and technology will find a solution to the problems. There are now several alternative ways of making electricity which do not produce carbon dioxide or nuclear waste: wind power, sea power (using either the waves or the tides), hydro-electric power (using the water in a dam) and solar power (using the sun's heat) are just a few ways which are now producing electricity. Car manufacturers are looking at water, sugar cane and electric batteries as ways of powering cars. Some car firms claim that by 2004 there will be fuel-cell cars on the market powered by the hydrogen from water. In the same way, recycling will enable the lifetime of many resources to be extended. Some cars are now made of almost 75 per cent recycled materials.

It is also possible to improve the efficiency and reduce the pollution caused by such things as cars. It would take 50 small cars being produced in 1999 to produce the same amount of pollution that one small car made in 1976. By 2010 the total tonnage of pollutants emitted by cars will be reduced by 75 per cent compared with 1992, even though the number of cars on the road will increase. Scientists are also working on using chemicals from plants rather than oil to produce such things as plastics.

Some people think an alternative lifestyle is necessary and they only use natural products (e.g. clothes made from cotton or wool), eat organic foods (foods grown without fertilisers or pesticides) and ride bikes instead of owning a car. They believe that if everyone lived in this way, environmental problems would disappear.

There are now many windfarms like this one in Cornwall producing pollution-free energy.

CHRISTIANITY AND THE ENVIRONMENT

> **God blessed them and said to them, 'Be fruitful and increase in number. Rule over the fish of the sea and the birds of the air and over every living creature that moves on the ground.'**

Genesis 1:28

> **When I consider your heavens, the work of your fingers ... what is man that you are mindful of him? You made him a little lower than the heavenly beings ... You made him rule over the work of your hands; you put everything under his feet**

Psalm 8:3–6

> The universe as a whole is a product of God's creative and imaginative will. All its parts are interdependent. Men and women are to be stewards and creators, not exploiters, of its resources, material, animal and spiritual. Christians must support those working for conservation and the development of more appropriate sustainable life-styles.

Christian Faith Concerning the Environment – Methodist Conference 1991.

Christians believe that God created the universe and everything in the universe.

The Bible says that when God created the universe, he saw what he had made, and saw that it was good. This means that Christians have to regard the whole of creation as a gift from God, to be used by humans in the way that God intended.

It is a basic belief of Christianity that God gave humans the stewardship of the earth and its resources. Stewardship means looking after something so that it can be passed on to the next generation. In the Parable of the Talents or Minas (Luke 19:11–26), Jesus taught that God expects humans to pass on to the next generation more than they have been given. Many Christians believe that this means Christians have a responsibility to leave the earth a better place than they found it.

To leave the earth a better place than they found it means that such Christians not only try to reduce pollution and preserve resources, they also try to improve the quality of life of the less fortunate. Christian stewardship, for them, means a sharing of the earth's resources for everyone, because of the teachings of Jesus in the Sermon on the Mount about sharing. So Christian stewardship can involve sharing the earth's resources more fairly and improving the standard of living in LDC's without causing more pollution.

> This Synod, affirming its belief and trust in God the Father who made the world ... urge Her Majesty's Government: to take all possible steps, both nationally and internationally, to establish a just and economical use of the Earth's energy resources, and to minimise the impact of consequential environmental pollution; to take positive steps to curtail damage to flora and fauna in this country, and to seek to extend such restraint elsewhere in the world.

Motion at the General Synod of the Church of England 1992.

All these teachings mean that Christians have a duty to share in and support the work of groups which try to reduce pollution and conserve resources. They also mean that individual Christians should be judging what they are doing in their life as an individual, by the standards of Christian stewardship. However, Christians believe God put humans in control of plants, animals and the earth and so in tackling environmental issues, human concerns cannot be ignored – for example shutting down a factory which causes pollution but employs three thousand people would not be a Christian solution. Christians believe that the problems of pollution and resources can be overcome by using their stewardship in God's way.

> Use of the mineral, vegetable and animal resources of the universe cannot be divorced from moral imperatives. Man's dominion over inanimate and other living beings granted by the Creator is not absolute; it is limited by concern for the quality of life of his neighbour, including generations to come; it requires a religious respect for the integrity of nature.

Catechism of the Catholic Church.

ISLAM AND THE ENVIRONMENT

Looking after the earth. Britain's first power station producing electricity from household rubbish.

Islam teaches that the universe and everything in it was created by one God and so there is a unity in all of creation. One of the most important Muslim beliefs is called Tawhid. This means that there is only one God and nothing is to be in any way connected with God, but it also means that there is a unity in creation. This unity between humans can be seen in the Muslim Ummah and in the way in which the universe runs on scientific laws which are a unity.

Many Muslims believe there is a balance in the universe which is revealed in this unity and in Surah 55. This belief in the balance of the universe is like extending the idea of an ecosystem to the whole universe.

Muslims also believe that God created Adam as his Khalifah (vice-regent or vice-gerent – someone who looks after things for you). This means that all Muslims are God's khalifahs who have to keep the balance of creation and look after the earth for God by following the way of life set out for Muslims in the Qur'an and the Shari'ah.

On the Day of Judgement, Muslims believe that they will be questioned by God on the way they have looked after the earth and the life on earth. Those who have polluted or misused God's gifts will not be allowed into heaven.

> Behold thy Lord said to the angels, 'I will create a vicegerent on earth.' . . . And He taught Adam the nature of all things . . . And behold, He said to the angels: 'Bow down to Adam.' And they bowed down: Not so Iblis: he refused and was haughty: He was of those who reject the faith.

Surah 2:30–34

> The sun and the moon follow courses exactly computed; And the herbs and the trees – both alike bow in adoration. And the firmament has He raised high, and He has set up the Balance in order that ye may not transgress balance.

Surah 55:5–8

> Behold in the creation of the heavens and the earth; in the alternation of the night and the day . . . in the rain which God sends down from the skies, and the life which He gives therewith . . . in the beasts of all kinds that He scatters through the earth; in the change of and the clouds . . . here indeed are signs for a people that are wise.

Surah 2:164

Muslims believe that this life is a test from God on which they will be judged at the end of the world. A major part of the test is looking after the environment in the way of Islam, and those who fail the test will be punished.

These teachings and beliefs of Islam mean that Muslims must be involved in removing pollution and be involved in the preservation of the earth's resources. However, Muslims believe that humans have been placed in charge of the earth's resources by God and so in tackling environmental issues, the effects on humans cannot be ignored.

The planet that we live on has been created by Allah and entrusted to mankind until the Day of Judgement. As His 'agents' on earth, we have the responsibility of looking after all of the other creatures, the plants, the atmosphere and everything else that surrounds us. It is important, therefore, for Muslims to play a leading part in the efforts to protect our environment. Life on earth is set up with natural balance and this is the key to our survival here.

What does Islam Say? Ibrahim Hewitt.

Islam's teaching on stewardship would make industry more environmentally friendly.

Judaism teaches that the earth belongs to God, and humans have been given the task of looking after the world for God. Jews believe that the way God gave humans control of the life of the planet in Genesis chapter 1 means that God wanted people to use the earth's resources wisely without either waste or misuse.

In building towns and cities, Jews have to follow a principle set down in Numbers 35:2 known as the migrash. This states that around every town there must be an area of open land. This land cannot be used in any way, not even for growing crops. So every town should have a pleasant environment with a surrounding parkland available for everyone to use for recreation. The Talmud suggests that the migrash should be surrounded by a ring of fruit trees.

Another important Jewish principle connected with the environment is that of never destroying anything needlessly. In biblical times when an army was attacking a town, it would lay siege to it by building a wooden wall so that no one could get out. Deuteronomy 20 says that Jewish armies are not allowed to cut down fruit trees for these walls. Later, rabbis took this to mean that Jews must never destroy things of the earth which are useful. Rabbi Joseph Schneerson told a story of how, when he was a boy and plucked a leaf off a tree, his father told him, 'Everything in nature is put there to serve God's purpose. We can use them for our needs, but we must be careful not to destroy things unnecessarily.'

JUDAISM AND THE ENVIRONMENT

> God blessed them (male and female) and said to them, 'Be fruitful and increase in number; fill the earth and subdue it. Rule over the fish . . . and the birds . . . and over every living creature'.

Genesis 1:28

> Command the Israelites to give the Levites towns . . . And give them pasture-lands around the towns . . . The pasture-lands around the towns . . . will extend fifteen hundred feet from the town wall.

Numbers 35:2

> **When you lay siege to a city for a long time ... do not destroy its trees by putting an axe to them ... Do not cut them down. Are the trees of the fields people, that you should besiege them?**

Deuteronomy 20:19

> **The earth is the Lord's, and everything in it, the world and all who live in it.**

Psalm 24:1

The respect for the land and for trees is shown in the special Jewish festival of Tu B'Shevat (New Year for Trees). This marks the new agricultural year in Israel at the end of January or the beginning of February. The New Year for Trees is celebrated by planting trees in areas where they are needed or by paying someone to plant one in a country where there is a lack of trees. It is also shown in the practice of Jubilee years. Leviticus 25 orders Jews that every 50 years they must not plant crops or harvest such things as fruit trees, nature must have a chance to recharge its batteries.

All these teachings and beliefs mean that Jews must be concerned about environmental issues and support the work of groups which are trying to stop pollution, end waste and use resources responsibly. However, like Christians and Muslims, they believe that human interests come first and that environmental issues cannot ignore human issues.

> People are beginning to regard themselves as just another part of the ecosystem. In Jewish thinking, such a view is misguided and dangerous. It leads to denying the supreme value of human beings ... For Jews, environmental concerns have to take into account the special place of humanity in creation. In other words, they have to have a moral dimension.

Arye Forta, *Moral Issues in Judaism.*

The Tees Barrage prevents both pollution and floods.

Hindus believe that there is a oneness in the universe and in nature which was created by God, and in which God is present. Most Hindus believe that there is an eternal law of nature and that the human soul should seek some form of union with this nature to find God and peace. This means that humans should not exploit or abuse nature, they should work with nature. Hindus have to work with the earth to produce crops and Hinduism teaches farmers that if they respect the earth, it will give them its treasures. The Hindu belief that God is a part of the earth he has created is a major reason for Hindus to respect the earth.

Hinduism also respects animal life. In his avatars, Vishnu appeared as a fish, a tortoise, a boar and a lion. Krishna was a cowherd. Many Hindus believe that they may have been animals in previous incarnations. So animals are respected and many Hindus believe that the teachings on ahimsa (non-violence) mean that they should be vegetarians refusing to take any form of life because they have respect for all life. Almost all Hindus regard the cow as sacred because of its connections with Krishna.

Forests are very special to Hindus. The third ashrama after the householder is the forest dweller (vanaprastha). The forests are pure nature untouched by humans and it is in living here that Hindus can find union with God. According to Hindu stories, Krishna spent much of his time in the forest which also makes them very special places. Certain trees are thought to be especially holy, for example, the banyan tree is thought to be holy because it was whilst sitting under a banyan tree that the Buddha became enlightened.

This is perhaps why the major Hindu green group, the Chipko, began with tree hugging. About 300 years ago, the followers of a Hindu sect led by a woman, Amitra Devi, decided to protect trees from the wood cutters by embracing the trees so that the woodcutters would harm them rather than the trees. In 1974 a group of village women in Garhwal hugged the trees which were about to be chopped down for a sports goods company as they knew it would ruin their lives. Some Hindu thinkers then remembered Jambeshwar who, in the fifteenth century had a dream that human beings would be destroyed because they had destroyed nature. So the Chipko (hug-the-tree) movement began, mainly with women, determined that India's rapid industrialisation should not destroy the environment.

These teachings and beliefs mean that many Hindus have a great respect for the environment. Nevertheless, some Hindus feel that as humans are the most advanced life-form, they have been given the right to use the earth's resources in any way they think is right. There is a lot of conflict in India today between those Hindus who want industrial progress regardless of the environment and those who think the environment must be protected from industry.

Indian civilisation has been distinctive in locating its source of regeneration, material and intellectual, in the forest, not in the city. India's best ideas have come where man was in communion with trees and rivers and lakes, away from the crowds. The peace of the forest has helped the intellectual development of man.

Rabindranath Tagore in Tapovana.

FACTFILE 63

HINDUISM AND THE ENVIRONMENT

The waters are the body of breath, and the moon up there is its luminous appearance. So, the extent of the waters and of that moon is the same as the extent of breath. Now, all of these are of equal extent, all are without limit. So those who venerate them as finite win only a limited world, whereas those who venerate them as infinite win a world without limit.

Upanishad 1:5:13

Peace of sky, peace of mid-region,
peace of earth, peace of waters, peace of plants.
Peace of trees, peace of all gods, peace of Brahman,
peace of the universe, peace of peace,
May that peace come to me.

Yajur-veda VI 36.17

May men and oxen both plough in contentment, in contentment the plough cleave the furrow. Auspicious furrow, we venerate you. We pray you, bless us and bring us abundant harvests.

Rig Veda IV.57

THE JEWISH NATIONAL FUND AND THE ENVIRONMENT

All religions have groups concerned with the environment. Much of the work of Christian Aid and Muslim Aid is concerned with environmental issues and the Hindu Chipko is an environmental group. The Jewish National Fund has specific concerns with pollution and resources.

Although not all Jews agree with the establishment of Israel, Jews from all over the world do regard Israel as a holy land and so they want to remove pollution and make sure the resources there are being used properly and carefully. The Jewish National Fund takes donations from Jews all over the world and uses them to improve the environment in Israel. It is a religious organisation following the mitzvot of Judaism.

Rolling back the desert in the northern sections of the Negev.

The work of the Jewish National Fund (JNF)

1 A major work of the JNF is to educate Jews outside Israel about the work of the Fund and collecting donations from them to use in Israel.

2 The JNF has planted 200 million trees. These trees not only reduce the greenhouse effect and provide outdoor recreation, they are actively used by the JNF to halt desertification. Much of Israel is next to desert land and the trees prevent the soil erosion which allows deserts to spread. Timna Park near Eilat on the Red Sea is a woodland park which JNF created out of the desert. However, forests can cause major ecological problems if a fire breaks out and so the JNF has developed techniques for preventing and controlling forest fires in hot climates.

3 The JNF has a very successful programme of rolling back the desert. It developed the technique known as 'savannisation'. This is based on planting things much further apart than normal and watering them by capturing the small amounts of rain and surface runoff in special holes. This has led to quite large areas of the northern Negev Desert (where annual rainfall is only 4–10 inches) becoming available for agriculture.

4 The JNF backs up its savannisation by building reservoirs and dams to capture the floodwaters of the desert areas. These can then be used to replenish underground aquifers, breed fish, halt soil erosion and irrigate fields for agriculture.

5 JNF also deals with health hazards such as waste dumps, landfills and abandoned quarries. It makes them safe by using proven environmentally friendly methods, and has created a unique landscape of groundwater pools in Nitzanim Park in the desert out of a dangerous abandoned quarry.

In all its work, the Jewish National Fund believes that it is putting into practice the teachings of Judaism on caring for the environment.

Factfile 59 Environmental issues

1 What is an ecosystem?

2 Make a list of things humans are doing which will damage the earth's ecosystem.

3 Explain why resources are likely to be a problem in the future.

4 Make a list of things people are doing to reduce the problem of resources.

5 Make a list of things people are doing to reduce the problem of pollution.

6 'People worry too much about the environment.'
Do your agree? Give reasons for your opinion, showing you have considered another point of view.

Factfile 60 Christianity and the environment

1 What is meant by Christian stewardship?

2 On what biblical teachings is stewardship based?

3 Explain how a parable Jesus told teaches Christians how to use the environment.

4 'If Christians took their religion seriously, there would be no environmental problems.'
Do you agree? Give reasons for your opinion, showing you have considered another point of view.

Factfiles 61, 62, 63 Islam, Judaism, Hinduism and the environment

1 Choose one religion and write down what it teaches about the correct use of the environment.

2 Give three reasons for these teachings.

Factfile 64 The Jewish National Fund and the enrironment

Explain how one religious agency is trying to improve the environment.

FACTFILE 65

WAR AND PEACE ISSUES

A shelter in Iraq, allegedly hit by American missiles in the Gulf War, 1991. There were 403 civilian casualties.

Most people approve of peace and disapprove of war. In 1945 the United Nations was established with the aim of keeping world peace and making sure that there was never another world war.

However, since 1945 there have been many wars which threatened to become world wars and in which both sides claimed to be justified.

The Korean War 1950–1953 was fought between the United Nations (mainly the USA) defending South Korea and North Korea and China. South Korea claimed she had been invaded, North Korea claimed she had been invaded.

The Vietnam War 1961–1975 was fought between North Vietnam supported by Russia and South Vietnam supported by the USA and Australia. North Vietnam claimed that the South was refusing to hold free elections to hold up the union of Vietnam which had been agreed in a peace treaty, while South Vietnam and the USA claimed to be preventing communist expansion.

In the Falklands War 1982, Argentina invaded the Falklands because they claimed Britain had no right to take them in 1830 and that Britain was refusing to negotiate. Britain sent a Task Force to recapture the islands because the people of the Falklands did not want to join Argentina and had a right to be defended.

There are many wars and war threatening situations at the moment in Kosovo, Bosnia, Israel, Eritrea, Rwanda, Kashmir, Iraq and many ex-members of the USSR. All these conflicts are caused by injustices of some kind. Often it is a race or religion being refused equal rights; or a country's borders not being respected; or wealth not being shared fairly; or democratically agreed decisions not being respected.

Many religious people feel that religions should be working to remove these causes of war. They feel it is scandalous that the world spends so much on armaments – if what is spent in one month on armaments were to be spent on world poverty, the problem of world poverty could be solved.

> To save succeeding generations from the scourge of war ... to reaffirm faith in fundamental human rights, to establish conditions under which justice and respect for the obligations arising from treaties and other sources of international law can be maintained and to promote social progress and better standards of life in larger freedom.

Extract from the *United Nations Charter* giving the reasons for its establishment.

All Christians believe that they are called to bring peace to the world. The message of the angels when Jesus was born was 'On earth peace to men' (*Luke* 2:14). Jesus said that those working for peace will be called sons of God. The New Testament is full of references to peace and the way in which Christians should be bringing peace and reconciliation.

The Christian Churches all make regular statements opposing war and encouraging their members to work for peace and stop war. However, they also realise that it is not always possible to avoid war. So although all Christians are against war and must work for peace, there are two different Christian attitudes to how Christians should behave if a war occurs.

1 Christian Pacifism

Pacifism means refusing to fight in wars and for the first 300 years of Christianity, Christians refused to fight in wars. The great Christian leaders (e.g. Origen, Tertullian and Cyprian) all argued that Christians must not be involved in war and must be pacifists. However, when the Roman Empire became Christian things changed so that by 438, the Emperor Theodosius could issue a law that only Christians could fight in the Roman Army.

In the twentieth century many Christians have become pacifists. They feel that the way modern warfare affects so many innocent people means that war can never be justified. There are many Christian pacifist groups, the largest being the Catholic group Pax Christi. The Quakers, Plymouth Brethren and Christadelphians are completely pacifist Churches. Some Christian pacifists not only refuse to fight in wars, they also refuse to be involved in any kind of violence and would not resist anyone who attacked them.

The reasons for Christian pacifism are:

- the teachings of Jesus about turning the other cheek and loving your enemies;

- the belief that peace will only come if people refuse to fight in wars;

- the horrible things that have happened to civilians in wars (especially the effects of the Hiroshima and Nagasaki nuclear bombs);

- the fifth commandment bans killing;

- Jesus stopped Peter from using violence when the soldiers came to arrest him with the words, 'Put your sword back in its place for all who draw the sword will die by the sword.'

FACTFILE 66

CHRISTIANITY AND WAR

> Blessed are the peacemakers, for they will be called sons of God.

Matthew 5:9

> I tell you, do not resist an evil person. If someone strikes you on the right cheek, turn to him the other also.

Matthew 5:39

> You have heard that it was said, 'Love your neighbour and hate your enemy.' But I tell you: Love your enemies and pray for those who persecute you.

Matthew 5:43–44

> How can Christians wage war, or even become soldiers in peace-time without the sword which our Lord has taken away.

Tertullian a second century Christian thinker.

> We utterly deny all outward wars and strife and fighting with outward weapons, for any end, or under any pretence whatever, this is our testimony to the whole world.

A Declaration from the Harmless and Innocent People of God called Quakers presented to King Charles II.

> He (Jesus) said to them, 'But now if you have a purse, take it, and also a bag; and if you don't have a sword, sell your cloak and buy one.'

Luke 22:36

> Everyone must submit himself to the governing authorities, for there is no authority except that which God has established. The authorities that exist have been established by God.

Romans 13:1

> Remind the people to be subject to rulers and authorities, to be obedient, to be ready to do whatever is good.

Titus 3:1

2 Christians and the Just War

St Augustine first put forward reasons which would justify Christians in fighting in a war. These were developed by St Thomas Aquinas into what is now known as the Just War. Most Churches agree that Christians are justified in fighting in a war if:

- the cause of the war is just (resisting aggression or removing a great injustice);

- the war is being fought by the authority of a government or the United Nations;

- it is being fought with the intention of restoring peace;

- it is begun as a last resort (all non-violent methods of ending the dispute have been tried and failed);

- there is a reasonable chance of success (lives should not be wasted if there is no chance of achieving the aims which justify the deaths);

- the methods used avoid killing civilians (though this would not involve such things as bombs aimed at armaments factories hitting hospitals accidentally);

- the methods used must be proportional to the cause (it would not be possible to justify destroying a country with nuclear weapons because it had invaded a small island).

These rules would justify fighting in such wars as The Falklands War, The Gulf War and fighting for the United Nations in Bosnia, Kosovo etc.

To the Christian serving in the armed forces of the 'Western democracies' there is the added assurance and comfort that their purpose is for defence and to maintain peace, not for selfish wars of aggression. The role of the Forces is almost entirely analogous to that of a police force ... Therefore a Christian can regard it as an honour, and as a duty to be faithfully followed, should God call him to serve in these armed forces.

From *Christians and War* published by the Officers' Christian Union.

Austrian soldiers behind the Russian Front, 1916. The Austrian invasion of Serbia began the First World War.

The reasons for the Christian just war theory are:

- St Paul said in Romans 13 and Titus 3 that Christians have to obey the orders of the government;

- Jesus never condemned the soldiers he met and actually commended the faith of the Roman Centurion in Luke 7;

- when Jesus was asked about paying taxes he said, 'Give to Caesar what is Caesar's' which must mean fighting in a just war ordered by the government;

- everyone agrees that a police force is needed to protect innocent people from criminals, in the same way an army ready to fight just wars is needed to protect innocent countries from criminal ones.

> As long as the danger of war persists and there is no international authority with the necessary competence and power, governments cannot be denied the right of lawful self-defence, once all peace efforts have failed.

Catechism of the Catholic Church.

The aftermath of rioting in the city centre of Londonderry after the Government allowed an Orange Order March to walk through the Nationalist Garvaghy Road in Portadown.

ISLAM AND WAR

Fight in the cause of God those who fight you, but do not transgress the limits; for God loveth not the transgressors.

Surah 2:190

Think not of those who are slain in God's way as dead. Nay, they live, finding their sustenance in the presence of the Lord.

Surah 3:169

Jaber reported that the Messenger of Allah said, 'War is a deception'.

Hadith quoted by Bukhari and Muslim.

Islam is not in favour of wars. One meaning of the word Islam is peace. The greeting used by all Muslims when they meet each other is 'salaam aleikum' – 'May peace be with you.' No true Muslim can possibly regard war as a good thing.

Ruqaiyyah Maqsood, *Teach Yourself Islam.*

Anas reported that the Messenger of Allah said, 'March in the name of Allah, and with the succour of Allah and over the religion of the Messenger of Allah! Kill not the emaciated old, nor the young children, nor the women'.

Hadith quoted by Abu Daud.

There is no idea of pacifism or turning the other cheek in Islam. The Qur'an encourages all Muslims to 'struggle in the way of Islam'.

The Arabic word for struggle is jihad which is often translated as holy war. However, Muslims believe in two forms of jihad, the greater and the lesser. The greater jihad is the struggle to make yourself and your society perfectly Muslim. This involves struggling with yourself and your desires, and not fighting. Lesser jihad is the struggle with forces outside yourself by means of war.

There are strict rules in Islam about when a war can be fought justifiably by Muslims:

- it must be fought for a just cause (either Islam is being attacked, or people are suffering an injustice, or in self-defence);

- it must be a last resort (all possible non-violent methods of solving the problem must have been tried);

- it must be authorised and led by a Muslim authority;

- it must be fought in such a way as to cause the minimum amount suffering;

- innocent civilians (especially the old, the young, and women) must not be attacked;

- it must be ended as soon as the enemy lays down his arms.

All Muslims would agree that if a war fulfils these conditions then a Muslim must fight in it. The reasons for this view are:

- the Qur'an says that Muslims must fight if they are attacked and Muslims believe the Qur'an is the word of God;

- Muhammad is the great example for Muslims in how to live and he fought in wars;

- Muhammad made many statements (hadith) about war which say that Muslims must fight in just wars;

- the Qur'an says that anyone who dies fighting in a just war will go straight to heaven.

Peace is the ideal for all Jews. Jews have always used 'Shalom alaykum' – 'peace be with you' instead of hello. The perfect society which Jews call the Messianic Age is thought of in terms of peace when 'they will beat their swords into ploughshares and their spears into pruning hooks. Nation will not take up sword against nation, nor will they train for war any more.' (Isaiah 2:4).

However, although Jews should seek peace, there is no concept of pacifism in Judaism. The Tenakh is full of accounts of wars in which God has been involved. So Judaism believes that it is acceptable to fight in wars under certain conditions. These are:

- if God has commanded it (as when God ordered Joshua to fight for the Promised Land);

- if they are attacked by an enemy;

- using a pre-emptive strike to stop an enemy from attacking you when they are about to attack;

- going to the aid of a country that has been attacked;

- any other type of war can only be fought if there are good reasons for it, if all peaceful attempts have been tried and failed and if it is approved by the supreme council of Jewish rabbis.

The first four types of war are called *milchemet mitzvah* and must be fought. The last type is called *milchemet reshut* and is optional. Wars fought to gain revenge or to take things from other countries are banned.

The reasons for Jewish attitudes to war are:

- a mitzvah is a command from God which all Jews have to obey so they have to take part in a milchemet mitzvah;

- in the Tenakh there are many accounts of how Israel was able to keep her independence by defending herself when attacked;

- the experience of Jews before and during the Second World War was that without a Jewish army to defend them, six million Jews were murdered by the Nazis in the Holocaust.

Even so, all Jews work for and want peace.

FACTFILE 68

JUDAISM AND WAR

> If your enemy is hungry, give him food to eat; if he is thirsty, give him water to drink.

Proverbs 25:21

> Turn from evil and do good; seek peace and pursue it.

Psalm 34:14

> The Torah was given to establish peace.

Midrash

> The sword comes to the world because of delay of justice and through perversion of justice.

Talmud

> The law will go out from Zion, the word of the Lord from Jerusalem. He will judge between many peoples and will settle disputes for strong nations far and wide. They will beat their swords into ploughshares and their spears into pruning hooks. Nation will not take up sword against nation, nor will they train for war any more.

Micah 4:3

HINDUISM AND WAR

> **Prepare for war with peace in thy soul. Be in peace in pleasure and pain, in gain and in loss, in victory or in the loss of a battle. In this peace there is no sin.**

Bhagavad Gita 2:38

> Non-violence is not a garment to be put on and off at will. Its seat is in the heart, and it must be an inseparable part of our being.

Ghandi

> In non-violence, the masses have a weapon which enables a child, a woman, or even a decrepit old man to resist the mightiest government successfully.

Gandhi

Hindus are dedicated to peace. At the end of all their prayers they pray for peace of mind and body, for peace from natural disaster and for peace from other people.

Hindus are very tolerant of other ideas and beliefs and many of the Hindu gurus of the past 100 years have been trying to show a peaceful way through the hatred and violence which religion can bring. However, not all Hindus are opposed to war and so there are two attitudes to war in Hinduism.

1 Pacifism and non-violence

Some Hindus believe that violence in any form is wrong and that Hindus should not take part in wars. India fought the only non-violent war in history when Gandhi led a war of independence against Britain in which he refused to allow any violence.

The reasons why they believe in non-violence are:

* the Hindu belief of ahimsa or non-violence is one of the moral codes of Hinduism;

* connected with ahimsa is the belief that to take life will darken your soul and put it further back on the way to moksha;

* Gandhi's idea of satyagraha (truth force) showed that pacifism can work as a way of removing injustice;

* the evidence of wars seems to show that they solve very little.

Gandhi.

2 The Hindu Just War

Perhaps the majority of Hindus believe that war is justified if fought in self-defence or to remove great injustice. India has an army which is fighting to keep Kashmir in India, and which fought to protect the Bangladeshis when they were being attacked by Pakistan. The Law of Manu sets out strict rules about war: civilians, women and children must not be harmed; anyone who surrenders, is disarmed or wounded must not be attacked; weapons must be such as to not cause unnecessary suffering (barbed, blazing or poisoned arrows are banned).

The reasons for this view are:

- in the caste system of Hinduism the second most important caste is the warrior caste whose caste duty was to defend society by war if necessary;

- the most popular Hindu holy book, the Bhagavad Gita, says that warriors must fight in just wars and that they need not fear killing because it is only the body that is killed, the soul cannot be harmed;

- there are many stories of battles in the Hindu Scriptures and Rama, the avatar of Vishnu, fought and killed the tyrant king Ravana.

So Hindus have a similar problem to Christians. Most probably accept the need to fight just wars, but a substantial minority is opposed to war in any form.

> **Think thou also of thy duty and do not waver. There is no greater good for a warrior than to fight in a righteous war. There is war that opens up the gates of heaven, Arjuna! Happy the warrior whose fate is to fight such a war.**
>
> *Bhagavad Gita 2:31–32*

Hindu soldiers use the teachings of the Gita to justify fighting in war.

QUESTIONS

Factfile 65 War and peace issues

1 Give three reasons for wars starting.

2 Name two wars fought since 1970.

3 Explain why wars would end if all countries followed the United Nations Charter.

Factfile 66 Christianity and war

1 What is pacifism?

2 Explain why some Christians believe they should be pacifists.

3 Give a Christian definition of a just war.

4 Explain why some Christians believe they can fight in just wars.

5 'No Christian should ever fight in a war.' Do you agree? Give reasons for your opinion, showing you have considered another point of view.

Factfiles 67, 68, 69 Islam, Judaism, Hinduism and war

1 Choose one religion and make a list of what is needed for its members to fight in a war.

2 Explain the reasons for their attitude to war.

3 'It is an insult to God for people to spend billions on arms when people are starving.' Do you agree? Give reasons for your opinion, showing you have considered another point of view.

RELIGION AND HOMOSEXUALITY

9

HOMOSEXUALITY – SEXUAL ATTRACTION (OFTEN CALLED ORIENTATION) TO THE SAME SEX.

HETEROSEXUALITY – SEXUAL ATTRACTION TO THE OPPOSITE SEX.

BI-SEXUALITY – SEXUAL ATTRACTION TO EITHER SEX.

HOMOPHOBIA – FEAR OR HATRED OF HOMOSEXUALS.

HOMOPHILE – LOVING THE SAME SEX.

Homosexuality has existed in all societies even though it has often been illegal. In Britain, homosexuality between males was a crime until 1967 when sex in private between two consulting adults (over 21) was made legal. In 1994 this was reduced to 18, but when the Government tried to reduce the age to 16 (the same as for heterosexual sex) it was rejected by the House of Lords.

When homosexuality was illegal, many people thought of homosexuals as evil and many thought homosexuality was a disease. Research by the medical profession has led to a very different view. It appears that at least five per cent of the population is homosexual, and doctors are agreed that they do not choose to become homosexual, with many thinking homosexuality has genetic causes.

There are, however, social pressures and it is still impossible to marry someone of the same sex and very difficult for same sex couples to adopt, even when they are trying to adopt children no one else will adopt. In October 1998 the French Socialist government suffered its first defeat when it tried to give same sex couples the same rights as heterosexual couples. Homosexuals have almost equal rights in the Netherlands where it is possible for same sex couples to marry.

There are homophobic groups in many countries and people who are openly homosexual are often attacked. The Nazis treated homosexuals in the same way as they treated Jews and gypsies, and several thousand homosexuals died in the concentration camps.

FACTFILE 70

THE SOCIAL BACKGROUND

In June 1998 the House of Commons voted by a 207 majority to reduce the legal age for male homosexual sex to 16, but in July 1998 the House of Lords voted by 190 votes to 122 to keep the age at 18.

The leader of the Greek Orthodox Church in Cyprus, Archbishop Chrysostomos made a violent speech attacking gays as 'depraved enemies of our nation'.

News report April 1998.

I accept that there may be limits to how far the law should attempt to enforce morality, but laws which are not founded on strong moral principles are, ultimately, empty vessels. From this broader perspective, I remain opposed to the lowering of the age of consent and take some comfort from the fact that very many people in our land share my sense of unease.

George Carey Archbishop of Canterbury July 1998.

CHRISTIANITY AND HOMO-SEXUALITY

> **Do not lie with a man as one lies with a woman, that is detestable.**
>
> *Leviticus* 18:22

> **For although they knew God, they neither glorified him as God nor gave thanks to him ... Therefore God gave them over in the sinful desires of their hearts to sexual impurity for the degrading of their bodies with one another ... Because of this God gave them over to sinful lusts. Even their women exchanged natural relations for unnatural ones. In the same way ... men committed indecent acts with other men and received in themselves the due penalty for their perversion.**
>
> *Romans 1:21–27*

> The number of men and women who have deep-seated homosexual tendencies is not negligible. They do not choose their homosexual condition; for most of them it is a trial. They must be accepted with respect, compassion, sensitivity.
>
> *The Catechism of the Catholic Church.*

There are several attitudes to homosexuality in Christianity. The main ones are:

1 The attitude of many evangelical Protestants is that homosexuality is a sin. There should be no homosexual Christians because the salvation of Christ can remove all sins. Such Christians run special prayer groups to give homosexuals the power of the Spirit to change their sexual orientation.

The reasons for this attitude are:

- the teachings of the Bible which condemn homosexuality (Leviticus 18:22, 20:13; Romans 1:26–7; 1 Corinthians 6:9; 1 Timothy 1:10);

- the evangelical belief of being born again in Christ which can remove all sins.

2 The Roman Catholic view is that homosexual orientation is not a sin, but homosexual sexual activity is a sin. The Catholic Church calls for homosexuals to live a celibate (not having sex) life and believes that the sacraments of the Church will help them to do this. At the same time, the Catholic Church condemns any form of homophobia.

The reasons for this attitude are:

- the same biblical teachings as the evangelical view;

- the tradition of the Church;

- the teaching of the magisterium as given in the new Catechism of the Catholic Church.

Bishop Holloway and Reverend Richard Kirker failed to persuade the Lambeth Conference to change the Church's attitude to homosexuality.

3 The Protestant view is that lifelong homosexual relationships are acceptable and homosexuals are to be welcomed into church, but homosexual relationships can never be equal to Christian marriage. Ministers/priests may have a homosexual orientation, but must not take part in homosexual sex.

The reasons for this attitude are:

- the Biblical passages need re-interpreting in the light of modern life just as those about women do;

- the same sex friendship of David and Jonathan and Ruth and Naomi show that same sex relationships are not totally condemned in the Bible;

- the Christian belief in love and acceptance means that homosexuals must be accepted;

- the Christian teaching on sex being restricted to marriage means that ministers/priests cannot have homosexual sex.

We do not reject those who believe that they have more hope of growing in love for God and neighbour with the help of a loving and faithful homophile relationship.

Church of England Report on Homosexuality.

4 The Liberal Protestant view is that these should be complete equality for homosexuals provided that the sexual relationship is a stable one and that the partners restrict sex to each other.

The reasons for this attitude are:

- Liberal Protestants such as Quakers believe inspiration comes from the Spirit as well as the Bible and if Christians feel the Spirit approves of their homosexuality, it cannot de denied;

- Liberal Protestants believe that the Bible needs to be interpreted in the light of modern knowledge and that the anti-homosexual texts in the Bible are a reflection of Jewish culture rather than the word of God.

In my dialogue with the Bible I ask, How can you be based on two events (the Exodus and the death and resurrection of Jesus) that are about transforming pain, suffering and death into life, liberation and healing, and yet call for the misery and death of lesbians and gay men?

GD Comstock, *Gay Theology without Apology.*

ISLAM AND HOMO-SEXUALITY

If two men among you are guilty of lewdness, punish them both. If they repent and amend, leave them alone; for God is oft-returning, Most Merciful.

Surah 4:16

Of all the creatures in the world will ye approach males, and leave those whom God has created for you to be your mates?

Surah 26:165–6

This perverted act (homosexuality) is a reversal of the natural order, a corruption of man's sexuality and a crime against the rights of females. The spread of this depraved practice in a society disrupts its natural life pattern and makes those who practise it slaves to their lusts, depriving them of decent taste, decent morals, and a decent manner of living.

Yusuf Qaradawi, *The Lawful and the Prohibited in Islam*.

Islam teaches that homosexuality is unnatural and sinful. Same sex relationships are against the laws of nature and the laws of God. Homosexuality is condemned by all the law schools which give a variety of punishments from whipping to death for those caught in homosexual relationships.

A number of hadith also show the Prophet Muhammad condemning those who dress as women or walk as women. Such behaviour is seen as dangerous as it threatens the family which is the centre of Muslim life.

The reasons for this view are:

- homosexuality is condemned by the Qur'an and the Qur'an is the final word of God which must be obeyed;

- the Prophet Muhammad condemned homosexuality and his was the last example given to Muslims;

- God laid down marriage between man and woman as the only lawful means of sex;

- the family is the centre of Islam and homosexual relationships deny the possibility of family life;

- sex is for having children and so homosexual sex must be wrong.

Although Islam is so clearly against homosexuality, many Muslim countries do have homosexuals who tend to be ignored because many Muslims do not believe there can be homosexuals in Islam. The fact that there are Muslim homosexuals in Britain can be seen in the recent setting up of a new counselling group for young gay and lesbian Asians in Britain.

MUSLIM LEADERS SUPPORT THE HOUSE OF LORDS ON HOMOSEXUALITY

News report April 1998.

JUDAISM AND HOMO-SEXUALITY

Jews would find it very hard to condemn homosexuals as such because they remember how homosexuals suffered alongside them in the Nazi death camps. Nevertheless, there are two different attitudes to homosexuality amongst Jews.

1 The Orthodox view is that homosexuality is a sin. A man feeling attracted to another man is no different from a married man being attracted to another woman. If he allows his feelings to result in sex, he has committed a sin. Most Orthodox Jews believe that homosexuality is developed mentally and can be cured by therapy. Although Orthodox Jews condemn homosexuality, they would never condemn homosexuals.

The reasons for this view are:

- homosexuality is forbidden in the Torah which is God's commands for Jews (Leviticus 18:22, Leviticus 20:13, Deuteronomy 23:18, Judges 19:1–30);

- Judaism restricts sex to marriage;

- it is the duty of every Jew to marry and have children to carry on the Jewish race which homosexuals cannot do.

2 The Liberal/Reform view is that homosexuality is now acceptable and there is a famous Reform rabbi, Rabbi Lionel Blue, who has declared his homosexuality. Liberal Jews in London run a Jewish Gay and Lesbian telephone helpline. Although these groups accept homosexuality, they still see heterosexual marriage as the ideal and the correct role model for children.

The reasons for this view are:

- Liberal Jews believe that the Torah and Tenakh needs to be re-interpreted in the light of the modern world;

- Jewish religious laws say you should treat others as you wish to be treated yourself and so homosexuals should be accepted;

- they are very aware of the close connections between homophobia and racism.

> I too knew what it was like to have no place in the happy family pictures which illustrated Sunday School textbooks. My gayness had saved me from self-righteousness. And this was useful because the number of outsiders was growing, and there was more spirituality among them than they realised.

Rabbi Lionel Blue, *A Backdoor to Heaven*.

> **If a man lies with a man as one lies with a woman, both of them have done what is detestable. They must be put to death.**

Leviticus 20:13

> **How the mighty have fallen in battle! Jonathan lies slain on your heights. I grieve for you Jonathan my brother; you were very dear to me. Your love for me was wonderful, more wonderful than that of women.**

King David speaking after the death of his friend Jonathan, *1 Samuel 1:25–6*

HINDUISM AND HOMO-SEXUALITY

There is in India a special caste of ascetics (people who give things up to dedicate themselves to God) called the Hijras. They consist of men who feel called to be castrated and then dress as women serving the Mother Goddess, Parvati. This sect reveal that sexuality is not necessarily easily defined in Hinduism and, according to G Herdt in *Same Sex Different Cultures*, recent research has shown far more homosexuality in India than was previously thought.

Nevertheless the majority of Hindus disapprove of homosexuality and see it as unnatural.

The reasons for this are:

- the Law of Manu only mentions and approves of heterosexual sex, therefore homosexuality must be wrong;

- all Hindus must pass through the second ashrama of householder, but homosexuals cannot be householders;

- if homosexuality prevents you from fulfilling your dharma, it will prevent you from attaining moksha and so should be avoided.

However, some Hindus believe that homosexual sex can be a way to God. There are many sculptures of homosexual sex (both male and female) in carvings on old Hindu temples in India and many Hindu homosexuals believe that homosexuality was thought of as holy and a way of communicating with God. They believe that homosexuals find it easier to spend time concentrating on God and trying to find moksha in other ways than the fulfilment of dharma.

> **I am the power of those who are strong, when this power is free from passions and selfish desires. I am desire when this is pure, when this desire is not against righteousness.**

Bhagavad Gita 7:11

> **When the tip of a hair is split into a hundred parts, and one of those parts further into a hundred parts – the individual soul, on the one hand, is the size of one such part, and, on the other, it partakes of infinity. It is neither a woman nor a man, nor even a hermaphrodite; it is ruled over by whatever body it obtains.**

Svetasvatara Upanishad 5:9–10

> The sexual life of the Hijras is complicated by the fact that they are strongly associated with the ascetic traditions of Shiva and Hinduism. They are communicants of the divine power of the Mother Goddess ... Therefore ideally the Hijras should not engage in sexual relations.

G Herdt *Same Sex Different Cultures.*

Ellen Degeneres and her same sex partner.

QUESTIONS

Factfile 70 The social background

1 When was homosexuality between adult males made legal in Britain?

2 What has medical research shown about homosexuality?

3 In which countries do homosexuals have equal rights?

4 What problems do homosexuals face in the United Kingdom?

Factfile 71 Christianity and homosexuality

1 Make a list of the differences between the four Christian views on homosexuality.

2 'You cannot be a Christian and a homosexual.'
Do you agree? Give reasons for your opinion, showing you have considered another point of view.

Factfile 72 Islam and homosexuality

1 Give an outline of the Muslim attitude to homosexuality.

2 Make a list of the reasons for this view.

3 Explain why some Muslims may not agree with this view.

Factfile 73 Judaism and homosexuality

1 Give an outline of the two Jewish attitudes to homosexuality.

2 Explain why Jews have different attitudes to homosexuality.

Factfile 74 Hinduism and homosexuality

1 What has recent research shown about homosexuality in India?

2 What is the attitude of the majority of Hindus to homosexuality?

3 On what is this attitude based?

4 Why do some Hindus disagree with this view?

FACTFILE 75

CONTRACEPTION

ARTIFICIAL METHODS OF CONTRACEPTION – METHODS SUCH AS CONDOMS, THE PILL, THE COIL

NATURAL METHODS – THE RHYTHM METHOD USING THE INFERTILE TIME IN A WOMAN'S MENSTRUAL CYCLE

STERILISATION – AN OPERATION TO MAKE IT IMPOSSIBLE TO CONCEIVE; THE REMOVAL OF THE OVARIES FOR WOMEN, A VASECTOMY FOR MEN

PROCREATION – HAVING CHILDREN

PROGENY – BABIES

Couples have always worried about producing too many children, but it was not until the end of the nineteenth century that medical technology introduced comfortable and reliable methods of contraception.

A contraceptive is something which allows sex to take place, but prevents conception from happening. They can be a physical barrier such as a condom, a drug such as the pill or the morning after pill, or an operation such as a vasectomy.

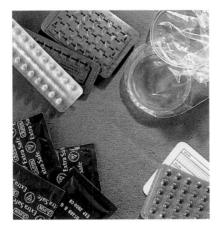

The use of condoms in the West has led to a stabling of the population so that the population is now rising very slowly. However, in less developed countries, the population is rising by as much as 3 per cent a year. This is placing great pressure on food supplies, health services and education and so many governments have massive family planning programmes to try to encourage their population to use contraceptives.

The rise of AIDS has led to a world-wide campaign for safe sex which involves the use of condoms to prevent infection being spread. Many doctors would regard it as foolish to have sex without a condom unless you could be 100 per cent certain that your partner had not had sex with anyone else.

For all these reasons, contraception is now encouraged everywhere and it is estimated that 90 per cent of the sexually active population of Britain uses contraception.

There are two completely opposite attitudes to contraception amongst Christians.

1 The Roman Catholic view is that any form of contraception other than the rhythm method is wrong. In 1930, Pope Pius XI condemned all forms of artificial contraception. In 1951, Pope Pius XII said that Catholics could use the rhythm method of restricting sex to the infertile period of the woman's menstrual cycle. This was re-affirmed by Pope Paul VI in *Humanae Vitae*, and Pope John Paul II has made several statements condemning artificial methods of contraception and affirming that Catholics can only use the rhythm method.

The reasons for this view are:

- sex was given by God in order for humans to reproduce and so every act of sex must be open to the possibility of a child being born;

- it is unnatural to use contraceptives and Christians should only do what is natural as nature is given by God;

- God said that humans should multiply and populate the earth;

- contraception encourages people to break God's laws about sex and is the major cause of promiscuity and diseases like AIDS;

- in the marriage service, a couple promise to have sex so that they can have children and so they should not use contraceptives.

2 The view of other Christians is that contraception of any form is all right as long as it is used to restrict the size of the family and not simply to stop having children altogether (although a few Christians would say this is acceptable).

The reasons for this view are:

- Christianity is about love and justice, and contraception improves women's health and raises the standard of living, education and health for children as there are fewer of them;

- God created sex for enjoyment and as a means of helping the relationship between a married couple and this is best done by allowing sex without the threat of pregnancy;

- there is nothing in the Bible to disallow contraception.

FACTFILE 76

CHRISTIANITY AND CONTRACEPTION

God blessed them and said to them, 'Be fruitful and increase in number; fill the earth and subdue it.'

Genesis 1:28

> Called to give life, spouses share in the creative power and fatherhood of God. Married couples should regard it as their proper mission to transmit human life.

Catechism of the Catholic Church.

> Every action which proposes, whether as an end or as a means, to render procreation impossible is intrinsically evil.

Catechism of the Catholic Church.

> With the use of contraception, the unitive and creative aspects of intercourse can play their full part in the healing and development of a marriage.

Statement by the Methodist Church in *What the Churches Say.*

FACTFILE 77

ISLAM AND CONTRACEPTION

Some Muslims are completely against contraception because they believe God intended sex for procreation and intended humans to have large families. They feel that contraception is unnatural.

However, the generally accepted Islamic teaching is that contraception is permitted for the following reasons:

- fear that pregnancy may endanger the life or health of the mother;

- fear that another child would place too great a burden on the finances of the family;

- fear that any children born would have genetically transmitted diseases.

Do not kill yourselves: for verily God hath been to you Most Merciful

Surah 4:29

God intends every facility for you; He does not want to put you to difficulties.

Surah 2:185

However, Islam does not allow contraception to be used to put off having children. Every Muslim couple is expected to have children, but may then use contraception to limit the size of the family. The reasons for this view are:

- there are several hadith which record the Prophet's approval of coitus interruptus (withdrawal before ejaculation) as a form of contraception;

- the Qur'an prohibits suicide and if pregnancy is likely to result in the mother's death if contraception is not used, not to use it would be like suicide;

- there are several verses in the Qur'an which say that God does not want to place extra burdens on his followers;

- Muslim lawyers agree that contraception is different from abortion.

If Allah wishes to create a child, you cannot prevent it.

Hadith reported by Abu Daoud, Ibn Majah, al-Nisai and al-Tirmidhi.

Contraception is not like abortion. Abortion is a crime against an existing being.

Imam Al-Ghazzali.

The preservation of the human species is unquestionably the primary objective of marriage, and such preservation of the species requires continued reproduction. Accordingly, Islam encourages having many children and has blessed both male and female progeny. However, it allows the Muslim to plan his family due to valid reasons and recognised necessities.

Yusuf Al-Qaradawi, *The Lawful and the Prohibited in Islam.*

There are different views in Judaism about contraception. Some Orthodox Jews think there should be no contraception other than the rhythm method, because God intended sex for the procreation of children. Reform Jews believe that any form of contraception is permitted because God allowed the use of intelligence and technology to prevent unwanted things happening.

The generally accepted view of contraception in Orthodox Judaism is that contraception is available after a couple have had at least two children (one boy and one girl) for the following reasons:

- there is a risk to the life or health of the mother if there is a pregnancy (this would permit the use of contraception before the birth of children);

- a further pregnancy would cause harm to the family's finances;

- there is a risk of future children having genetic diseases.

It is the female who uses contraception.

The reasons for this view are:

- the Tenakh says that God wants humans to populate the earth;

- Jewish marriage is intended to carry on the Jewish people;

- God intended sex to be enjoyed by a married couple not to make hardships;

- the sanctity of life teachings mean that contraception should be used to save life;

- The Torah teaches that male seed is sacred.

JUDAISM AND CONTRACEPTION

> For this is what the Lord says – He who created the heavens, he is God: he who fashioned and made the earth, he founded it; he did not create it to be empty, but formed it to be inhabited.

Isaiah 45:18

> For this reason a man will leave his father and mother and be united with his wife, and they will become one flesh.

Genesis 2:24

> Look upon our affliction and plead our cause, and redeem us speedily for thy name's sake; for thou art a mighty Redeemer . . . Grant a perfect healing to all our wounds; for thou, almighty King, art a faithful and merciful Physician.

From the Afternoon Service.

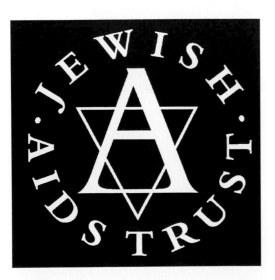

Following the principle that the sanctity of life is paramount, the Jewish AIDS Trust advises the use of condoms to prevent HIV transmission.

FACTFILE 79

HINDUISM AND CONTRACEPTION

> **When a man deposits the semen in a woman . . . it becomes one with the woman's body as if it were part of her own body.**

Aitareya Upanishad 2:2

> **As a man leaves an old garment and puts on one that is new, the Spirit leaves his mortal body and then puts on one that is new.**

Bhagavad Gita 2:22

There is a wide range of views among Hindus about contraception.

Some Hindus do not believe in any form of contraception as they believe sex is only intended for the procreation of children.

Some Hindus only permit certain forms of contraception e.g. the pill and vasectomy, as they think anything which kills the sperm is banned by the Hindu teaching on ahimsa (non-violence).

The generally accepted Hindu view is that contraception is a good thing and Hindu religious leaders have supported the Indian Government in its campaigns to use birth control as a means of halting India's population explosion. The reasons for this view are:

- children should be a joy and not a burden;

- humans have free will and so they should use their intelligence and technology to improve life and to make sure that population does not exceed food supply;

- contraception is different from abortion and does not involve violence;

- the soul does not enter the body until after conception and so souls cannot be affected by contraception.

Most Hindus limit the size of their families by contraception.

Infertility has become much more of a problem in the western world in recent years with as many as 10 per cent of couples in the UK estimated to have fertility problems.

Medical technology has provided many solutions which are known as **embryo technology:**

IN-VITRO FERTILISATION (IVF) – WHEN AN EGG FROM THE WOMAN IS FERTILISED OUTSIDE THE WOMB USING EITHER THE HUSBAND'S OR A DONOR'S SPERM AND THEN REPLACED IN THE WOMB

ARTIFICIAL INSEMINATION BY HUSBAND (AIH) – WHEN THE HUSBAND'S SPERM IS INSERTED INTO HIS WIFE BY MECHANICAL MEANS

ARTIFICIAL INSEMINATION BY DONOR – WHEN AN ANONYMOUS MAN DONATES SPERM WHICH IS INSERTED MECHANICALLY INTO THE MOTHER

EGG DONATION – WHEN AN EGG IS DONATED BY ANOTHER WOMAN AND FERTILISED BY IVF USING THE HUSBAND'S SPERM AND THEN PLACED IN THE WIFE'S WOMB

EMBRYO DONATION – WHEN BOTH EGG AND SPERM COME FROM DONORS AND ARE FERTILISED USING IVF

SURROGACY – EITHER WHEN THE EGG AND SPERM OF WIFE AND HUSBAND ARE FERTILISED BY IVF AND THEN PLACED INTO ANOTHER WOMAN'S WOMB; OR WHEN ANOTHER WOMAN IS ARTIFICIALLY INSEMINATED BY THE HUSBAND'S SPERM. IN BOTH CASES, AFTER THE BIRTH THE WOMAN HANDS THE BABY TO THE HUSBAND AND WIFE.

All of these are now being used by couples in Britain supervised by the Human Fertilisation and Embryology Authority, though there have been many arguments about their morality.

This is clearly an issue for religion as many of the opponents of fertility treatments have accused doctors of playing God. However, to the parents concerned, fertility treatments have been regarded as a miracle.

FACTFILE 80

RELIGION AND INFERTILITY

Sarah and Peter's triplets conceived by IVF.

CHILDREN MAY GET RIGHT TO FIND DONOR PARENTS

Newspaper headline from 20.10.98 when the Government ordered an investigation into sperm and egg donation which is now running at 2000 births a year.

I f the semen of a man is placed in an artificial womb . . . the action is permissible and . . . all orders applicable to a father and child will be applicable to them . . . Making the semen of a husband reach the womb of his wife artificially is permissible and the child thus born is like all other children.

Articles of Islamic Acts, Imam Al-Khoei.

Christian viewpoints

There are two very different Christian views on infertility.

1 The Roman Catholic view is that life is given by God and that no one has a right to children. Although the Catholic Church feels great sympathy for the childless who want children, it only allows methods which do not threaten the sacredness of life and in which sex acts are natural. This means that all embryo technology is banned for Catholics, as IVF involves fertilising several eggs some of which are thrown away or used for experimentation. Also all forms of artificial insemination or surrogacy involve masturbation by the male which is a sin for Catholics.

T echniques that entail the disassociation of husband and wife, by the intrusion of a person other than the couple . . . are gravely immoral. These techniques infringe the child's right to be born of a father and mother known to him and bound to each other by marriage . . . Techniques involving only the married couple . . . are perhaps less reprehensible yet remain morally unacceptable. They dissociate the sexual act from the procreative act.

The Catechism of the Catholic Church.

2 The other Christian Churches allow IVF and AIH, but have major concerns about all other embryo technology. They feel that it is good to use technology to provide couples with the joy of children, but that all the other methods involve problems of who the parent is and could lead to problems for the children in terms of their identity and also legal problems about exactly who the parents are. All Christians believe God intended children to have only one mother and father.

T he Division of the Methodist Church responsible for advising the Church on medical ethics has accepted for the time being the scientific judgement that remedies for human infertility, and for certain genetic diseases and handicaps, would be greatly assisted if research on embryos not required for artificial insemination continues to be carried out . . . that investigation . . . is permissible up to fourteen days.

Statement of the Methodist Church in *What the Churches Say.*

Muslim viewpoints

Most Muslims accept IVF and AIH when couples are having fertility problems, as these are simply using medicine to bring about the family life which all Muslims are expected to have. However, they disapprove of all the other types of embryo technology because they deny a child's right to know its natural parents and they are very similar to adoption which is banned in Islam.

Jewish viewpoints

Having children is so important in the Jewish faith and for the preservation of Judaism that rabbis are very supportive to couples who are having fertility problems. IVF, and AIH are accepted by all Jews and many accept egg donation. Some feel that the egg must be donated by a Jewish woman to make the baby Jewish, but others think that upbringing is enough. AID is seen as a form of adultery and so is not allowed. Surrogacy is not allowed as it is felt that whoever gives birth to a child is the mother.

Hindu viewpoints

Most Hindu couples long for children, especially a son. The Law of Manu encourages infertile couples to adopt from a relative. This works well in India where there are large families, however, few Hindu families in Britain would be prepared to do this and so Hindu couples are turning to embryo technology. Hinduism has no problems with IVF and AIH. However, AID and embryo donation are not allowed because caste is passed down through the father. Most Hindus disapprove of egg donation and surrogacy, but some would allow it if there are strict safeguards and all other methods have been tried.

Sarah and Peter have triplets who were conceived by IVF treatment after years of trying to have children.

When Sarah was asked how she and Peter felt when they were told they were unlikely to have children she replied, 'As a woman I felt a failure and excluded. I had a sense that there was this special person whom I desperately wanted to meet, but wasn't being allowed to. As a wife, I felt I was a dud.' Peter, despite genuinely wanting children, was able to be more philosophical. He said, 'As a couple, we felt we were ready to move on to the next stage of our lives, but were suspended in childlessness. We felt real sadness.'

When asked how they felt when offered fertility treatment, Sarah said, 'We never felt it was wrong. We never thought it was tampering with the course of nature or against the will of God. We simply felt I had a medical condition that was in no way my fault and which needed treatment. We were delighted and optimistic when first offered treatment. The period of treatment was a real emotional roller coaster. As the years dragged on and we entered the realms of high-tech treatment, I became very worried that it wouldn't work.'

As far as life being parents is concerned, Sarah said, 'Life as parents is exhausting and hard work, but excellent. We feel a sense of the future and continuation. The babies give us a lot of happiness and laughter, which outweighs all the worry and loss of our relatively hedonistic lifestyle. They are a real gift to us.'

An interview with the parents of the triplets on page 143.

QUESTIONS

Factfile 75 Contraception

1 What is contraception?

2 What is the difference between artificial and natural methods of contraception?

3 Give two reasons for the popularity of contraception.

Factfile 76 Christianity and contraception

1 What are the different Christian attitudes to contraception?

2 Make a list of the reasons for the Roman Catholic view.

3 Make a list of reasons for the Protestant view.

4 'Contraception is a gift from God to make life better.'
Do you agree? Give reasons for your opinion, showing you have considered another point of view.

Factfiles 77, 78 Islam, Judaism and contraception

1 Choose one religion and give an account of the generally accepted attitudes to contraception.

2 Make a list of the religious reasons on which these attitudes are based.

3 Explain why some Muslims/Jews disagree with this attitude.

Factfile 79 Hinduism and contraception

1 What are the three Hindu attitudes to contraception?

2 Make a list of the religious reasons for the main attitude.

3 Explain why some Hindus disagree with the main attitude.

Factfile 80 Religion and infertility

1 What is embryo technology?

2 What methods of embryo technology cause most problems for religion?

3 Give two reasons why these methods cause problems.

4 What are the Christian views on embryo technology?

5 Explain why Christians have different attitudes to embryo technology.

6 Choose one religion other than Christianity and outline its attitude to embryo technology.

7 'If God wants us to have children, we will have them: there is no need to use technology.'
Do you agree? Give reasons for your opinion, showing you have considered another point of view.

RELIGION AND SCIENCE

Many people think that science and religion are totally different from each other. They think that science is about facts, and religion is about unprovable things which cannot happen. Because of these ideas, they think that scientists have nothing to do with religion. However, this is not true. There are scientists who have been led to believe in God through science and many religious people think that science and religion are two ways of looking at the same facts.

1   Christianity, Islam, Judaism, Hinduism, Buddhism and Sikhism all claim that the universe has been made by God in some way, and that if the universe is investigated, it will be seen that there are laws of nature which show that God has designed everything. In the same way, science claims that the universe works on laws, on principles which work whether humans know them or not. Science is based on everything having an explanation, and religion says that God is the explanation.

2   Science says that objects in the world can be affected by forces which cannot be detected by human senses e.g. gravity, magnetism. Science says that these unseen forces can only be observed by their effects. In the same way, religion claims that human beings can be affected by a force which cannot be detected by human senses, a force they call God. This unseen force, God, can only be observed through its effects on human lives.

FACTFILE 81

HOW SCIENCE AND RELIGION ARE CONNECTED

> The heavens declare the glory of God; the skies proclaim the work of his hands.

Psalm 19:1

> Behold! In the creation of the heavens and the earth; in the alternation of the night and the day ... In the rain which God sends down from the skies and the life which he gives therewith to an earth which is dead; in the beasts of all kinds ... here indeed are signs for a people that is wise.

Surah 2:164

Einstein.

3 Science and religion often use the same methods. Scientists see things happening in the world, then work out a theory to explain why they are happening and then test out that theory by experiment. For example, if they observe that a candle goes out when it is covered, they will work out a theory that burning requires air, then carry out experiments which remove the air when things are burning, to see whether they can burn without air.

In the same way if someone claims to be a prophet sent from God, religious experts would test the claim by experiment: how does the prophet's teaching and lifestyle compare with previous prophets, does the prophet affect people's lives by making them better people, does the prophet bring people to God.

4 Most religions would say that a study of science leads to an awareness of God and many scientists are deeply religious because their science has brought them into contact with God. They look at the order and design in such things as DNA and think it is too complicated and beautiful to be an accident. Many mathematicians think that the whole universe works on mathematical principles which they discover through research. If the principles are there waiting to be discovered, they must have been put there by God.

Other religious scientists say that science is based on everything having an explanation and so the universe must have an explanation, and the only explanation of why the universe is here is God.

5 Although science is more easy to prove than religion, both science and religion rely on belief and experience. A scientist believes that things do not happen by chance and that everything has an explanation and then tests that belief by experience of science. A religious person believes in God and then tests that belief by their experience of life.

The beauty and order of the solar system lead many astronomers to believe in God.

Cosmology and evolution

Cosmology is the word given to the study of the origin and structure of the universe. Evolution is the name given to the theory that life on earth began as very primitive basic life forms such as amoeba, and developed through the process of natural selection (if there is a mutation which is better adapted to its environment, this mutation will reproduce and become a new species) to animal and plant life. It also claims that humans evolved from animals.

SCIENCE AND CREATION

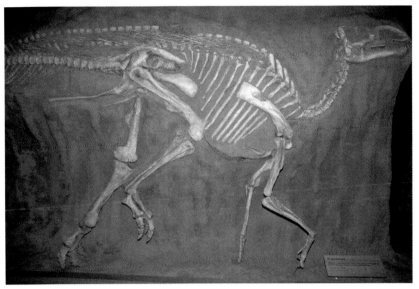

Many scientists claim dinosaurs are evidence for the scientific cosmology.

The scientific cosmology

This claims that:

- the universe began about 15 billion years ago with a Big Bang when the matter of the universe became so compressed that it produced a huge explosion;

- as the matter flew away from the explosion, the forces of gravity etc. joined some together into stars;

- about 5 billion years ago the solar system formed;

- 4.5 billion years ago primitive life began on earth;

- this life evolved and about 2.5 million years ago, humans first appeared.

This cosmology seems to have no need for God. Also, if it is true, it means that the Jewish, Christian and Muslim view that God created everything in six days is wrong. It causes few problems for Hinduism, Buddhism and Sikhism as they believe that life is cyclic (goes on and on, changing but never beginning or ending) and so the Big Bang could keep happening (the universe dies and is reborn just like souls).

The biblical cosmology

According to the Bible, Genesis 1, God created the whole universe in six days in the following way:

Day 1   heaven and earth, light and dark.

Day 2   the separation of the earth from the sky.

Day 3   the dry land, plants and trees.

Day 4   the sun, moon and stars.

Day 5   fish and birds.

Day 6   animals and humans.

This is so different from the scientific cosmology, that they cannot both be true and Jews and Christians have to try to work out what they believe about creation. There are several views.

1 Creationism

This view says that science is wrong and the Bible is right. It claims that all the evidence there is of the Big Bang and evolution can be explained by the effects of Noah's flood (which must have totally changed rock formations) and the Apparent Age Theory.

Apparent Age Theory claims that if you accept the Bible view, then when Adam was made the earth was six days old, but to Adam it would have looked billions of years old because trees would have been created with rings showing them as hundreds of years old; the Grand Canyon would have looked two billion years old when it was one second old and so on.

2 Conservatism

This view says that both science and the Bible are correct. The main points of the Bible story fit with science. One of God's days could be millions or billions of years. They claim that Genesis 1:3 'God said, "Let there be light" ', is a direct reference to the Big Bang and that the order of creation in plants, trees, fish, birds, animals, humans is the order of science.

Most Muslims would say something similar about the Qur'an and it's teachings of a six day creation.

3 Liberalism

This view says that the Bible is not meant to be regarded as true, it is a story told to give the vital piece of truth that God created everything. Many liberal Christians and Jews are scientists who claim that because the scientific cosmology is so remarkable it means it was the way God used to create humans. They claim this because:

- the Big Bang had to be at exactly the right micro second. If it had been too soon it would have been too small to form stars, if it had been too late, everything would have flown away too fast for stars to form;

- the way stars are formed out of hydrogen and helium and by nucleic reactions produce carbon and oxygen, which are spread around the universe by exploding supernovae, this implies a creator organising things;

- the way in which life on earth requires carbon to be able to bond with four other atoms and water molecules could not have happened by chance.

So they feel that the Big Bang and evolution could only have happened if God made them happen and they claim that even at the moment of the Big Bang, the nature of matter and the laws of science mean that humans were bound to appear.

> The Big Bang theory implies the act of a God who intended to create beings like us.

Stephen Hawking *A Brief History of Time*.

> What is revealed of the divine in the human life of Jesus is also to be discerned in the cosmic story of creation.

J Polkinghorne *Science and Creation*.

> The point is that, for the existence of any forms of life that we may conceive, the necessary environment, whatever its nature, must be complex and dependent on a multiplicity of coincident conditions, such as are not reasonably attributable to blind forces or to pure mechanism.

FR Tennant quoted in *The Existence of God* ed. J Hick.

John Polkinghome, a university scientist led by science to become a Church of England priest.

QUESTIONS

Factfile 81 How science and religion are connected

1 Explain the similarities between what science and religion think about the nature of the universe.

2 State what is similar about the way religion and science test things.

3 Explain why some scientists believe in God.

4 'Science has disproved religion.'
Do you agree? Give reasons for your opinion, showing you have considered another point of view.

Factfile 82 Science and creation

1 Give a definition of cosmology.

2 Give an outline of the scientific cosmology.

3 Give an outline of the biblical cosmology.

4 Explain why some people think that Big Bang and Evolution disprove religion.

5 'No one can believe in the Genesis story of creation today.'
Do you agree? Give reasons for your opinion, showing you have considered another point of view.

Useful addresses

BBC Religious Broadcasting
New Broadcasting House
Oxford Road
Manchester M60 1SJ

Board of Deputies of British Jews
Woburn House
Upper Woburn Place
London WC1H 0EP

CAFOD
2 Romero Close
Stockwell Road
London SW9 9TY

Catholic Truth Society
38–40 Eccleston Square
London SW1V 1PD

Channel 4 TV
60 Charlotte Street
London W1P 2AX

Christian Action on Poverty
Central Buildings
Oldham Street
Manchester M1 1JT

Christian Aid
PO Box 100
London SW1 7RT

Christian Ecology Group
c/o Mrs Joan Hart
17 Burns Gardens
Lincoln LN2 4LJ

Christian Education Movement
Royal Buildings
Victoria Street
Derby DE1 1GW

Churches Commission for Racial Justice
Inter-Church House
35–41 Lower Marsh
London SE1 7RL

Church of England Information Office
Church House
Dean's Yard
London SW1P 3NZ

Commission for Racial Equality
10–12 Allington House
London SW1E 5EH

EXIT (Voluntary Euthanasia Society)
13 Prince of Wales Terrace
London W8 3PG

ISKCON (International Society for Krishna Consciousness)
10 Soho Street
London W1V 5FA

Islamic Foundation
Markfield Dawah Centre
Ratby Lane
Markfield
Leicester LE67 9RN

Islamic Relief
19 Rea Street South
Birmingham B5 6LB

Islamic Vision
481 Coventry Road
Birmingham B10 0JS

Jewish Care
221 Golders Green Road
London NW11

Jewish Education Bureau
8 Westcombe Avenue
Leeds LS8 2BS

Life
Life House
Newbould Terrace
Leamington Spa
Warwickshire CV32 4EH

Muslim Aid
PO Box 3
London N7 8LR

Muslim Educational Trust
130 Stroud Green Road
London N4 3R2

National Abortion Campaign
Wesley House
4 Wild Court
London WC2B 5AU

Office of the Chief Rabbi
Adler House
Tavistock Square
London WC1H 9HN

Ramakrishna Vedanta Centre
Unity House
Blind Lane
Bourne End
Berkshire SL8 5LG

Salvation Army Headquarters
101 Queen Victoria Street
London EC4P

The Swaminarayan Hindu Mission
Shri Swaminarayan Mandir
105–119 Brentfield Road
Neasden
London NW10 8SP

Tearfund
11 Station Road
Teddington
Middlesex TW11 9AA

Union of Liberal and Progressive Jews
Montague Centre
109 Westfield Street
London W1P 5RP

World Jewish Relief
Drayton House
30 Gordon Street
London WC1H 0AN

How Religion and Life covers the short courses

This matrix summarises the GCSE RE short courses and shows how Religion and Life covers the syllabuses.

TOPIC	LONDON A1	LONDON A2, 4, 5	NEAB D	SEG 480	MEG B	WJEC
Marriage and family life	✓	✓	✓	✓	✓	✓
Social harmony	✓	✓	✓	✓	✓	✓
Believing in God	✓	✓	✓	✓	✓	✓
Matters of life and death	✓	✓	✓	✓		✓
Religion and the media	✓	✓		✓		
Religion, wealth and poverty	✓	✓	✓	✓	✓	✓
Religion and the environment	✓	✓	✓	✓	✓	✓
War and peace			✓	✓	✓	
Religion and homosexuality		✓	✓		✓	✓
Religion and medical issues		✓				✓
Religion and science			✓	✓	✓	✓

INDEX

Abortion 83, 84
   Christianity 84, 85
   Islam 85
   Judaism 86
   Hinduism 86
Adultery 16
   Christianity 20
   Islam 24
   Judaism 27
   Hinduism 30

Bhagavad Gita 13, 74, 77, 82, 86, 128, 129,
   136, 142
Bible – nature of 7, 8
Bible references 20, 22, 23, 32, 33, 42, 50, 70,
   71, 74, 78, 79, 84, 85, 89, 99, 100, 114,
   123, 124, 131, 139, 147, 149

Catechism of the Catholic Church 7, 20 23,
   32, 33, 43, 57, 99, 100, 114, 125, 132,
   139, 143
Christian Aid 107–109
Cohabitation 16
   Christianity 20
   Islam 24
   Judaism 29
   Hinduism 30
Contraception 138
   Christianity 139
   Islam 140
   Judaism 141
   Hinduism 142
Cosmology 149–151
Creation 67, 149–151

Deforestation 111
Divorce 17–19
   Christianity 22
   Islam 26
   Judaism 29
   Hinduism 31
Documentaries 95, 96
Double-effect 83
Dramas (television) 97

Employment
   by gender 41
   by ethnicity 49
Environment 111–113
   Christianity 114

Islam 115, 116
Judaism 117, 118
Hinduism 119
work of the JNF 120
Euthanasia 87, 88
   Christianity 89
   Islam 90
   Judaism 90
   Hinduism 90
Eutrophication 111
Evil and suffering (problem of)
   69

Family life 18, 19
   Christianity 32, 33
   Islam 34, 35
   Judaism 36, 37
   Hinduism 38, 39
Film 97

God (nature of)
   Christianity 7
   Islam 9
   Judaism 11
   Hinduism 13
God (reasons for believing in) 62–68
Greenhouse effect 111

Hadith 34, 35, 44, 90, 101, 126, 134, 140
Homosexuality 131
   Christianity 132, 133
   Islam 134
   Judaism 135
   Hinduism 136

Immortality 78, 79, 81
Infertility 143, 145
   Christianity 144
   Islam 144
   Judaism 145
   Hinduism 145

Jewish National Fund 120
Just War 123, 126, 129

Law of Manu 39, 45, 103
Law (UK)
   abortion 83
   divorce 17
   euthanasia 87

Law (UK) – *cont.*
   homosexuality 131
   infertility 143
   marriage 17
   race relations 49
   religion 55
   sex equality 41
Life after death
   Christianity 78, 79
   Islam 80
   Judaism 81
   Hinduism 82

Marriage 16
   Christianity 21–23
   Islam 24–26
   Judaism 27–29
   Hinduism 30, 31
Meaning of Life 68, 79, 80, 81, 82
Miracles 66
Moksha 13, 30, 74, 82, 128, 136
Moral Issues 7, 9, 11, 13, 15
   in television soaps 96, 97
Multi-ethnic society 47–49
Multi-faith society 55, 56
Muslim Aid 101

Orthodox Jews 12, 27, 29, 37, 45, 135

Pollution 111, 112
Poverty
   World 104, 105, 107, 108
   UK 106
Protestants 7, 8, 20, 22, 42, 57, 83, 84, 132,
   133, 143

Qur'an
   nature of 9
   references 24, 26, 34, 35, 44, 52, 58, 71, 73,
     80, 85, 90, 101, 114, 125, 126, 134, 147,
     149

Race Relations Act 48
Racial Harmony
   Christianity 50, 51
   Islam 52
   Judaism 53
   Hinduism 54
Radioactive pollution 112
Reform Jews 12, 27, 28, 29, 45, 135
Religous attitudes to other faiths 60
   Christianity 57
   Islam 58
   Judaism 59
   Hinduism 59
Religious broadcasts 92–96
Religious experience 64–66

Religious upbringing
   Christianity 62
   Islam 63
   Judaism 63
   Hinduism 64
Resources
   problem of 112
   proper use of 113, 114
Responses to evil
   Christianity 70, 71
   Islam 72
   Judaism 72, 73
   Hinduism 74
Resurrection 78–81
Roles of men and women 41
   Christianity 42, 43
   Islam 44
   Judaism 45
   Hinduism 46
Roman Catholics 7, 8, 21, 23, 42, 43, 57, 83,
   132, 139, 143

Salvation Army 106
Sanctity of Life 76, 77
Science and Religion 67, 68, 147, 148, 149,
   151
Sex 16
   Christianity 20
   Islam 24
   Judaism 27
   Hinduism 30
Shari'ah 9, 10, 80, 85, 115
Soaps 96, 97

Talmud 11, 27, 102, 127
Tenakh
   nature of 11
   references 27, 28, 36, 37, 45, 53, 59, 73, 77,
     86, 107, 117, 118, 127, 135, 141, 147,
     149

Upanishads 13, 82, 119, 136, 142

Vedas 13, 119

War 122
   Christianity 123, 124
   Islam 125, 126
   Judaism 127
   Hinduism 128
Wealth and Poverty
   Christianity 99, 100
   Islam 101
   Judaism 102
   Hinduism 103
World Development 104, 105
Worship on television 94, 95